THE WORLD WAR II HISTORY JOURNALS 1939 - 1945

A Chronological Timeline of WW2

Liam Dale

The History Journals

The HISTORY Journals

CONTENTS

WORLD WAR II HISTORY JOURNALS: 1939

The history of the world has rarely been peaceful and sadly at one time or another there have been battles fought just about everywhere, and most countries have experienced warfare. Whether fighting to form new nations, make laws, or oppose them, the instinct to go to war is a fundamental part of human nature.

Yet despite modern day attempts to have nations live together in peace and harmony, the great battles of the past have frequently become the stuff of folklore and legend. The Ancient Greeks famously went to war over the beautiful face of Helen of Troy, the Romans built an empire based on war, and even the tales of Robin Hood are deeply rooted in the Crusades, which saw Richard the Lion Heart fighting a Holy war for control of the city of Jerusalem.

However, the true cost of war fought long ago is often forgotten, as it was the victors who inevitably wrote the history books, but more recent conflicts have actually been subject to much greater scrutiny. From the 20th Century onwards we have been better able to see warfare from all sides and the two World Wars, which shaped the globe as we now know it, between 1914 and 1918, and 1939 and 1945 have a great deal to teach the human race.

Ignoring the lessons of history has been the cause of many conflicts, none more so than World War II, and with the help of incredible archive footage and the development of photography it is possible to build an accurate picture of how this war started, was fought, and concluded.

Throughout this series of journals released to acknowledge 80 years + since the beginning of WW2, we will be looking at the seven years of that conflict on an annual basis. The conflict, the build up to war, the major battles, the strategies and technological developments, the effect on civilians and most importantly of all we'll consider the role of the soldiers, sailors and airmen who gave their lives fighting for the freedom of others.

The statistics from World War II to this day, still make alarming reading as it's generally accepted that this global conflict caused the deaths of over fifty million people, with two thirds being civilian, killed as a result of bombings, large-scale massacres, starvation and hardship. However, unlike the Great War of 1914 to 1918, which saw over ten million military deaths and many more million civilian casualties, the Second World War is rarely seen as mindless slaughter.

The future of just about every nation and the way the world was governed depended upon the Allies winning the war, because if the outcome had swung in favour of Adolf Hitler and his Axis powers of Evil, the cost to humanity would have been even greater.

The war was not just a battle between nations and people, but of hearts and minds. On one side you had leaders who were obsessed by dogma, with little or no respect for humanitarianism or personal freedom. The big three were Adolf Hitler's Nazi Germany, Imperial Japan, and Benito Mussolini's Fascist Italy. The notions of compliance, loyalty to the state and a ruthless affinity for world domination obsessed all three nations.

These were the Axis powers and their worldview for a stronger future was one based on inferior and superior races. In fact these were political ideologies in stark contrast with what the majority of right-minded people and governments believed.

The forces that joined together to ensure that this new Axis world order would never become a reality were known as The Grand Alliance, more commonly referred to as the Allies. Some of the nations this collaboration included were Great Britain and the Commonwealth, France, the Low Countries, the Soviet Union and then a little later the United States of America.

All the nations that fought against the Axis powers did so not only to stop Hitler's new world order but for the principles of freedom, democracy and human values. This is perhaps difficult to reconcile with the Soviet Union's brutal dictator Joseph Stalin, who was extremely vicious throughout his regime, with a hatred of bourgeois freedom and parliamentary democracy, and he could never by any stretch of the imagination be considered a humanitarian.

Yet despite Russia being controlled by Stalin and agreeing to a non-aggression pact with Germany in the build up to the war, Adolf Hitler made a huge tactical error turning the Russians against the Nazis, and the Soviet Union played as big a part in the defeat of Hitler as any of the other Allied nations.

War was officially declared on Germany on the third of September 1939, two days after the German army invaded Poland, but the storm clouds of war had been gathering for many years before this. Europe had never enjoyed a real, lasting peace since the end of The Great War twenty-one years earlier. It had been described as the war to end all wars, but evidently, it was not.

Throughout this time of uneasy peace, the more liberal western powers had missed several opportunities to put an end to Germany's crusade for world domination, but hindsight is sadly only ever of any use, after the event.

After the armistice that ended the Great War in 1918 much of Germany felt that their homeland had been completely humiliated and stripped of any national pride. At the signing of the Treaty of Versailles, on the 28th of June 1921, Germany was held officially responsible for the war.

The American President, Woodrow Wilson joined with the British Prime Minister, Lloyd George and the French Premier, Georges Clemenceau to come up with a series of measures to maintain peace and security for the future and claim reparations from Germany to compensate the loses the Allies had suffered. However, although the Treaty of Versailles was not solely to blame for Germany's unrest, it was viewed by many as a harsh settlement that would inevitably hurt the German people rather than the military leadership responsible for starting the war in the first place.

In the Grand Hall of Mirrors at the Palace of Versailles, which modern day visitors can enjoy in perfect peace and tranquillity, Germany was forced to give up valuable industrial land, including the Rhineland, to France, Belgium, Poland, Lithuania, Denmark, and Czechoslovakia. The German politicians also agreed to complete disarmament and the abolition of all military service, the Army, Navy and Air Force. But back in Germany this earned them the title the "November Criminals" and there was nationalist feeling abroad that the politicians had stabbed the military in the back.

Through the 1920s the German people faced terrible hardships as a result of the reparations the country was forced to pay, and they were constantly looking for a way out of poverty, caused by high levels of unemployment. It was in this volatile climate that Adolf Hitler steadily rose to power, promising the people of Germany the hope of salvation.

Adolf Hitler was born in Braunau am Inn, in Upper Austria on the 20th of April 1889. Although Austrian, he served as a German soldier in World War I, and was awarded the Iron Cross, First Class. After the war he entered politics as a fierce German patriot and he infiltrated the German Worker's Party, influencing other like-minded soldiers to rise up against the Treaty of Versailles.

Hitler was already a renowned orator and he soon had a wide following, blaming the Jews and the Communists for Germany's terrible predicament. Soon he seized power as Fuhrer of the party and changed the name to the National Socialists, otherwise known as the Nazis.

The German people were living in desperate poverty so when Hitler spoke of the great need for Lebensraum, or living space, they hailed him as a hero. One of the outcomes of the First World War was the disintegration of the German Empire and had the Treaty of Versailles been effective it would not have been possible for Germany to claim any of this land back. In Hitler's semi-autobiographical book "Mein Kampf", which he wrote while serving a prison sentence for a failed attempted coup, he addressed the people of Germany and promised the return of what had been lost.

This was without doubt a man with big ideas for his adopted homeland, no matter what the consequences, and as he systematically removed any opposition the outside world simply looked on.

Hitler was obsessed by Lebensraum and he was determined to rebuild the German Empire and expand it further still, and world events were about to take a turn that would make his case for German supremacy even stronger.

In America on October the 29th 1929, the Stock Market on Wall Street crashed, beginning the period known as the Great Depression. This resulted in poverty and unemployment for millions worldwide, and Germany, already suffering terrible hardship, was one of the hardest hit countries. In a very short time extreme nationalist movements became very popular amongst the people, with Adolf Hitler leading the way, promising that he was Germany's salvation if they followed his direction.

When people are struggling for survival, they will often look to powerful and influential figures to lead them. Hitler was a prolific speaker who could rally a crowd to the point of hysteria and by 1932 the Nazis were the largest single party in German Reichstag. He knew how to manipulate people and was an excellent propagandist and outstanding political campaigner. Hitler blamed Germany's economic hardships on the Jews and the Treaty of Versailles and as he become ever more powerful, being appointed the Chancellor of Germany in 1933, he was now in a position to address both issues.

The warning bells were starting to ring amongst the architects of the Treaty of Versailles, but although unsettled, they chose not to take any action. Even when Hitler openly announced that he was breaking the treaty in March 1935, he was met with little resistance.

Hitler decided that Germany was no longer going to abide by the restrictions on armed forces and he started rebuilding the German military machine immediately. Britain and France were appalled by his actions and condemned them severely, however they did nothing to stop Hitler and simply watched as his empire grew.

Nazi Germany under Hitler's command, over the course of the next four years, continued to break every promise made in the aftermath of World War I. However, no matter what the Germans did during this period it would seem that the other nations around the world would do little to stop him. Matters worsened when Germany's President Hindenberg died in August, at which point Hitler seized that office too, making his position unassailable.

This in effect meant that Hitler could demand almost anything of his army, no matter how ruthless or cruel. Rights were being stripped from the Jewish community, and the Nazis opened the first concentration camp, as the Gestapo were placed above the law. A terrifying New World Order was becoming a reality, and something was going to have to be done if Hitler was going to be stopped.

Driven by the desire for power and land, in the March of 1936 Hitler broke the Treaty of Versailles once more, by marching his troops into the then demilitarized Rhineland. Astonishingly, yet again all the western world did was to look on in disbelief at what was happening.

Many governments couldn't face the prospect of another war and thought it better to allow Hitler to take the land in the hope that this would be enough. As soon as Hitler's troops arrived, they began to rebuild fortifications, so that even if neighbouring France decided to take any action, the German army would be ready.

The prelude to war was now well underway and in Britain, the voice of Winston Churchill could be heard warning the nation about the threat Adolf Hitler was now posing. Some thought that when Prime Minister Stanley Baldwin retired in May 1937, Churchill might succeed him, but the far less controversial Neville Chamberlain was selected instead.

Even though wisdom is meant to come with age, Chamberlain was sixty-eight at the time, he proved to be far too trusting when it came to judging character. He believed Hitler could be appeased and made every effort to avert war, whatever the cost, but with nothing to stop him Hitler continued to build his military machine.

Not content with the Rhineland, in the March of 1938 Hitler forced neighbouring Austria into unification with Germany. The growing Nazi party actually had quite a strong following in Austria and when the authorities tried to resist the Anschluss, Hitler simply ordered his army to cross the border into Austria, where they encountered no resistance.

After Austria, Hitler looked towards Czechoslovakia, and the rest of the world finally realised he would never stop in his quest for global domination, unless they acted. The threat of a Second World War was imminent, but Neville Chamberlain made one last bid to appease Hitler.

At the end of September 1938, Chamberlain, along with Daladier of France, the Italian dictator Mussolini and Hitler met in Munich and a treaty was signed granting part of Czechoslovakia to the Germans, if it was agreed that Nazi aggression would be halted.

Neville Chamberlain returned triumphant, famously waving a piece of paper bearing Hitler's signature. The waiting crowds cheered as war with Germany appeared to have been averted. Chamberlain was given a royal welcome at Buckingham Palace, and when he eventually returned to even bigger crowds at number 10 Downing Street, he confidently predicted that the Munich Pact would ensure 'peace for our time'.

And so we come to 1939 and the realisation that Hitler's word was anything but honourable. On the 15th and 16th of March the Nazis marched into Prague and seized the rest of Czechoslovakia. It was now apparent that Hitler could not be trusted, and war with Germany was inevitable.

Just as Winston Churchill had warned, the German army were now better prepared for conflict because from 1936 onwards they had been building and stockpiling armaments. In fact in this short but crucial space of time they had built almost ten thousand more aircraft than Great Britain and over eighteen thousand more than France. Hitler really was gearing up for war.

To make matters worse Hitler was now looking Eastwards and the threat to neighbouring Poland was very real indeed. But Hitler knew that before he invaded Poland, he had to make sure that the Soviet Union would not attack him, so he signed a non-aggression pact with Russia.

Hitler and Stalin agreed to invade Poland together and split up Poland's territories, and although Hitler intended to also advance on the Soviet Union, his empire was not yet powerful enough to do so, and for the time being he preferred to have the Russians on his side.

Hitler assumed that he would now meet with little opposition as he planned his invasion of Poland. The western forces had done hardly anything so far to stop him, so why should now be any different. To an extent he was right; the British and French governments tried their hardest to persuade the Poles to make concessions to Germany, and Chamberlain even considered that some of Hitler's demands were reasonable for Poland.

But there was unrest in Britain as more people and politicians realised that Hitler should no longer be appeased and war with Germany was the only honourable course of action. On August the 25th 1939 Britain signed a formal alliance with Poland, promising to come to the country's aid if Hitler invaded.

Hitler had first planned to invade Poland on August the 26th, however word of this new alliance may well have made him more cautious, especially as his ally Benito Mussolini announced that Italy would remain neutral if war broke out. Mussolini and his army were not ready for conflict yet and the Italian dictator even attempted to set up an international peace conference on the 31st August. The French were also obliged to come to Poland's aid in the event of a German invasion and they welcomed Italy's peace talks, but Hitler ignored them all, and a day later ordered his troops to storm across the border into Poland.

Under the agreement of the Anglo-Polish pact and a threat of revolt in the House of Commons, Chamberlain was reluctantly forced to give Hitler an ultimatum, pull out of Poland by 11.00am on the 3rd of September or face the consequences.

The deadline passed with no word from Germany, and with a heavy heart, just a quarter of an hour later, Chamberlain did what he had to do. In a radio broadcast at 11.15am on the BBC, Prime Minister Chamberlain informed the nation that as Hitler had failed to remove his troops from Poland, Britain was now at war with Germany.

For the second time in twenty-one years, Germany was at war with her European neighbours, and on that fateful Sunday morning a conflict began that would result in the Second World War.

Almost immediately after Chamberlain's announcement was made, a siren was sounded in London, and many people hurried to find shelter from what they thought was the first attack by the Nazis. Luckily, this was a false alarm, although over the course of the conflict that dreadful monotone sound would be heard throughout the country, spreading fear and panic into people everywhere, as the true horrors of war became all too real.

Although too little, too late, Chamberlain's government set about stepping up the war effort, especially in the light of the huge loss of life suffered in the First World War. The British wanted to be certain that everything was done to make sure that the conflict ended quickly and with minimal loss of life.

From March onwards, after Hitler had advanced into Czechoslovakia, a programme had been drawn up in Britain for the mass evacuation of children from London and other major cities likely to be attacked by German bombers, to the relative safety of the countryside.

By the end of 3rd September, it's believed that nearly one and a half million evacuees had been moved. Two thirds of this number were children and their teachers, while the remaining third were women with babies or expectant mothers.

The evacuation process was managed extremely efficiently, each child was labelled with its name, address, and school number. They all had to carry a gas mask, toothbrush, comb, soap, towel, night wear, handkerchief, spare underwear and if they had it, an overcoat. All the children were sent to railway stations where they were issued with a blank ticket, as it was not known yet where their destination was going to be.

The criteria were to get them out of the cities as quickly as possible before the anticipated air raids began and it must have been a very traumatic experience for all concerned, not only for the evacuees. The people of rural Britain were expected to open up their homes to the children of complete strangers, but even at this early stage, everyone was prepared to do their duty for King and Country.

However, the first attack would not be an air raid over a city, it was many miles away out at sea. Within a few hours of war being declared the Germans made their first strike against the Allies. At 7.45pm on the 3rd of September, a German submarine torpedoed the SS Athenia, an ocean liner bound for Montreal.

One hundred and twelve people perished that night as the first deaths of a result of the war were counted.

But it wasn't all bad news on 3rd September for the people of Britain. Winston Churchill, who had so fiercely opposed the appeasement of Hitler, was appointed as first Lord of the Admiralty.

There was great relief nationwide at this announcement and it is said that the Admiralty even flashed a jubilant message to the Royal Navy that simply said the words 'Winston is back'.

Winston Churchill was born in November 1874 at Blenheim Palace near Oxford. He was the son of Lord Randolph Churchill, an aristocrat and a politician and Winston followed in his father's footsteps into Parliament. When the message said, "Winston is back" it was because he had been First Lord of the Admiralty at the time of the First World War.

Always outspoken, Winston had made his fair share of enemies in the House of Commons, and when he was involved in the orchestration of the Battle of Galipoli, a total military disaster for the Allies in World War I, he was made the scapegoat, and stripped of his office. No doubt this contributed to parliament's dismissal of his warnings about Hitler, but when he returned to the Admiralty in 1939, the people of Britain were very glad this great statesman was at the forefront of the war effort.

After a flurry of activity as curfews and nightly blackout precautions were put in place, nothing much seemed to happen immediately. The German bombers didn't fly over London, the British armed forces weren't sent straight to Poland and no shots were fired in anger.

It was all rather confusing and many of the children who had been evacuated, returned home again. In fact the biggest casualties came as a result of the blackout, because road accidents doubled as cars were not allowed to use their headlights, and there were no streetlamps so many pedestrians were injured as a result of falls.

Nevertheless, strict rules were put in place for the blackout and Air Raid Precaution Wardens, better known as ARPs were appointed. They were mostly volunteers who enforced the blackout, and later when the bombings started, staffed the air raid shelters as well.

Early in 1939, the Military Training Act had been passed which required all young men between the ages of 20 and 22 to do six months military training and once war had been declared a further National Service (Armed Forces) Act followed, with men between 18 and 40 liable for call up to the army, navy or airforce. Also many people signed up voluntarily throughout 1939 and gradually Britain became better prepared for what lay ahead.

Yet all seemed strangely peaceful for a country at war. Apart from gardens being dug up so that people could start growing their own vegetables, and air raid shelters being built, the streets of Britain looked the same as they always had, and the events of the last quarter of 1939 became known as the Phoney War.

The Americans, who for the time being remained neutral, were also wondering what was happening in Europe between these warring nations. However, it wasn't only the British and French who were under prepared for war at this stage in the proceedings. Surprisingly, although the Germans were better placed than their enemies, they didn't attack immediately when war was declared because there was still much to be done if the Nazi fighting machine was going to be able to carry out Adolf Hitler's orders.

His revolutionary military tactics required large numbers of troops to maintain offensive lines so very little was left to use elsewhere. Blitzkrieg, or lightning strike as the term translates, utilised the German tanks to invade Poland in great numbers and at incredible speed, sometimes covering up to one hundred miles a day. The tanks stormed across the landscape, backed up by the mobile infantry in trucks and supported overhead by the screaming dive-bombers of the Luftwaffe.

The British couldn't help Poland until they'd built up sufficient armaments, so production went into overdrive. If the RAF were sent to fight straight away then there would be no protection for the United Kingdom and although the government were duty bound to help, they still had to ensure that their home territory was safe from attack first.

Ironically, the French did have the troop numbers to be able to make a difference. They actually had ninety infantry divisions, compared to Britain's ten, and if they had combined with Polish troops at the start of the German offensive, they would have out numbered the invaders by forty divisions. The Germans might well have been overcome if the French army had been ready, because on the German French border only twenty-three divisions had been left for defence, with the Blitzkrieg demanding so many men.

Unfortunately, the French army, despite being so large, was slow to mobilize because the majority of the men were conscripts, working nine to five jobs in times of peace but ready to take up arms when needed. It would take two weeks for these men to leave their jobs, put on their uniforms and prepare for war, and they were just too slow.

In those two short weeks the German tanks and their Blitzkrieg strategy resulted in the occupation of Poland, at which point they sent their troops back to defend their German French border. It was a crucial fortnight that gave Adolf Hitler a distinct edge.

To make matters worse for the besieged people of Poland, two weeks after Germany's invasion the Russians invaded, as agreed in the German-Soviet alliance to take complete control of the country. There was little the Allies could do and the few French that had fought their way into Germany were ordered back to guard the Maginot Line, a defensive boundary made up of trenches, pillboxes and large guns that ran along France's frontier with Germany on the west side. All the French could do was watch and wait as the Germans and Russians between them crushed Poland.

Meanwhile the British had opted for a rather different tactic to fight back with. The RAF were embarking on extremely successful raids all over Germany, making drops on Hamburg, Bremen, and the Ruhr. However these forays failed to cause one single civilian casualty. The RAF were not dropping bombs on the people; their hulls were filled with over twelve million propaganda pamphlets.

The hope was that these leaflets would influence the German people to demand a peaceful settlement to the conflict, pointing out that Hitler was to blame for their country going to war. However, from the mid 1930s onwards, the population of Germany had themselves suffered at the hands of Adolf Hitler, and an atmosphere of terror kept many quiet, who would have otherwise spoken out against the Fuhrer.

Needless to say, the leaflets did very little to sway German opinion and in Britain, Winston Churchill vehemently objected, saying they were nothing but a waste of time and resources. However, the pamphlet drops did help in another way, giving the young British pilots vital target practice, because it wasn't going to be long before these airmen would be flying back over Germany with a much deadlier cargo.

But for the time being Britain was not prepared to begin bombing civilian areas and neither for that matter were the Luftwaffe. At this stage propaganda was everything and as the war had only just begun no government wanted to be blamed for thousands of civilian deaths. All the protagonists knew that the first to begin bombing civilian targets could potentially face a huge backlash in public opinion against them.

The German troops on the ground in Poland had other ideas and weren't anywhere near so squeamish when it came to civilian deaths, and they soon established a reputation for brutality. On the 4th of September over one thousand civilians at Bydgoszcz (bidgoshe) in Poland were captured, lined up against a wall and shot dead.

The Nazi officers claimed that *'brutal guerrilla war had broken out everywhere'*, but the sad truth was that the German officers and soldiers thought that war allowed such brutality, and in seven years of conflict, many more horrific crimes against humanity would be committed.

As the autumn of 1939 gave way to winter, the war continued to remain largely isolated, contained well away from the public eye. Also there were many countries with such pressing domestic concerns that they kept out of the fray, no matter how many lives were being lost in Poland. Most of Europe remained neutral; some had vital business with Germany and chose not to put fragile economies at risk.

Even America, Britain's most significant ally in World War I, with their vast army and huge natural resources of raw materials, wanted to stay out of a war so far from home. The American President, Franklin D Roosevelt thought it in his country's best interests to stay on the sidelines. In a radio discussion on the 9th of September he said that he had seen war and hated it, and that he would make every effort to keep the United States out of it.

Good news did come to the Allies from America's neighbour, when the Canadians declared war on Germany on the 12th of September. The Prime Minister, Mackenzie King, wanted Canada to be a part of the war effort, however he chose not to bring in conscription. Canadian troops had fought and perished in World War I and Mackenzie King didn't want to force anyone to die in a war on foreign soil. Yet, what Canada would supply in the form of raw materials, food, air training facilities, industry and convoy escorts would be of vital importance.

This assistance from Canada, although essential to the overall war effort, like the rest of the Ally's early campaign against Hitler, was of little help to the people living in the Polish capital, Warsaw. On September the 27th those who had bravely defended the city for so long, surrendered as German troops poured into what was left of one of the world's loveliest old cities. It is estimated that more than 40,000 people were killed or injured in the offensive and Warsaw was left in ruins. The Germans needed to take complete control of the land and air, because bombing the city was the only way to destroy Warsaw.

They couldn't get their tanks through the defensive traps put in place by Poland's citizens and with hand-to-hand combat, the defending Polish army proved altogether tougher than the Germans had ever thought possible. The only way they could overcome the Poles was to bomb them into the ground, with no regard whatsoever for human life, whether military or civilian.

Matters were also made much worse, because there was no food, water, power, or gas in the city. The deadly disease, Typhoid, had taken hold of Warsaw and the consequences were horrific. A few days after the surrender, Germany and the Soviet Union created the 'German-Soviet Boundary and Friendship Treaty', which divided up Eastern Europe into zones of either Nazi or Communist influence. The first part of Hitler's blueprint for the control of Europe had been successfully implemented, seemingly with very little resistance from the Allies.

At this early stage in the war, Neville Chamberlain's war cabinet was still more concerned about forming alliances than fighting, and even Hitler was using this lull before the storm to build up his resources.

Yet again Hitler extended his hand in peace to France and England on the 29th of September, saying that he had no fight with them; all he wanted was the acknowledgement of the new powers in Europe. But the Allies were now wise to Hitler's manipulating and would not fall for his false promises again. Hitler could not be trusted so therefore he had to be stopped. Although the Allies wanted to quickly put an end to Hitler's power, the phoney war continued to persist.

The RAF maintained their propaganda pamphlet drops while

half a million French and British soldiers sat tight on the Maginot line waiting for orders to fight. The Allied leaders believed that they were still not ready to start firing, as they wanted to be sure they were fully primed. Unfortunately for the Allies, they were unaware that the Germans were also significantly under prepared for any counter attacks.

Because of all the troops needed in Poland, they had seriously weakened their defensive borders with France, and they didn't have a single tank on the Siegfried line, the name given to the German defensive border, which ran along the boundaries with Western Europe. Also there was only enough ammunition to last about three days.

With the benefit of hindsight and wisdom after the event, the beginning of the war for many historians has been regarded as a wasted opportunity for the Allies, at a time when they had a good chance to overcome the Nazis. However because the British and French governments were unaware of how poor the German defences were; in fact the Allies thought that the Siegfried line was incredibly well prepared against attack, the Phoney War continued.

If Prime Minister Chamberlain and his French counterpart had made the decision to send the Allied troops to Germany to fight, there might have been no need for a seven-year conflict. This proves how important quality Intelligence is to a successful war campaign. It is in fact as vital as ammunition and military personnel. Only reckless leaders would send their troops into a battle where nothing was known of the enemies' tactics or numbers, and at this stage for the Allies, caution was very definitely their watchword.

Because of the months wasted with appeasement tactics during the late 1930s, the Allies needed this time to really work out what they wanted to do next, how to mobilize the troops and determine Hitler's plans. While this was going on most of Western Europe, on the land at any rate, seemed strangely at peace. However, out at sea it was already a very different story.

As we saw earlier, the first casualties occurred out in the Atlantic Ocean, just hours after war was declared, and the fighting on the high seas continued throughout the early months of war. The notorious German U boats, through the latter stages of 1939, appeared to rule the waves and everyday the reports came in of Allied shipping being sunk by these deadly submarines. HMS Courage, HMS Ark Royal, HMS Nelson, HMS Gypsy and numerous other ships and cargo carriers had been targeted by the U boats, and although not all were sunk, the Germans were successfully managing to control movement between countries by sea.

The non-aggression pact between Hitler and Stalin had allowed the Nazi occupation of Poland, but towards the end of the year the Russian Red Army had an agenda of its own and began an attack on neighbouring Finland.

The Fins were drastically outnumbered and the Russians, adopting a similar form of offensive to the Germans, had hoped to take this Nordic country in a matter of weeks. But just like the Poles, the Fins had other ideas. They were an extremely tough fighting force and were determined to give their all in the battle against the Red Army, which would last several months. Even as winter set in, they were not deterred by the dreadful conditions.

The Finish army used troops on Skis, camouflaged in white to fight Stalin's army, and they inflicted terrible casualties on the Russians, proving that in the conflict ahead nothing was ever going to be a foregone conclusion.

Apart from the action out at sea, throughout Eastern Europe

and Finland, 1939 would end rather inconclusively for the Allies, as the people of Britain struggled to get used to the blackout and living without their children, and many wondered if the nation really was at war. Apart from the occasional German plane shot down over British soil and the news of the war at sea, very little had seemed to happen in the first four months of the conflict. However, looking at the bigger picture things were gearing up on all sides and this was just a prelude to the appalling bloodshed yet to come. All the people of Britain had to do was look to the east and see the burning embers of the destroyed cities of Warsaw in Poland and Helsinki in Finland to understand that the fighting and suffering was already happening.

From a military perspective, at this stage Adolf Hitler and his Axis powers of evil certainly appeared to have the upper hand as the Allied forces quite literally watched and waited.

Nevertheless, despite the fact that the fighting had not yet reached Britain, the people were rallying together to make sure that no matter how many battles Hitler won he would never win the war.

As people sat down to their Christmas dinner, soldiers awaited orders and evacuated children put on a brave face for their first festive season away from home and they all listened to King George VI making a poignant Christmas radio broadcast to the nation.

As 1939 drew to a close, the King spoke of the spirit of freedom and the need to risk all for its preservation, and over the coming years many of the people of Britain would pay the ultimate sacrifice, before the war fought in the name of freedom would be won. The New Year would bring with it the fall of Norway, the Low Countries and France, and see the Battle for Britain begin, and as this series of The War Journals continues you can follow the incredible stories of strategy, sacrifice, stoicism, and courage in the next chapter, 1940.

WORLD WAR II HISTORY JOURNALS: 1940

As the clock struck midnight on December the 31st 1939, and the world welcomed in the New Year of 1940, people everywhere awaited the outcome of this second global conflict of the 20th Century, with bated breath.

1939 had been a turbulent year, and since war had been declared on Adolf Hitler and Nazi Germany on September the 3rd, nobody could predict what the future might hold. Great Britain, under the leadership of Prime Minister Neville Chamberlain had worked tirelessly to appease Hitler and come to a peaceful compromise over his rebuilding of the German Empire, despite the fact that he was violating all the restraints of the Treaty of Versailles, placed on Germany after the First World War.

Precious months had been lost by the Allies to prepare for the Nazi onslaught, and although there was something of a lull before the storm afforded the Allies by what was described as a "Phoney War" between September and December 1939, they had a great deal of catching up to do. If anyone had been in any doubt about the seriousness of the threat to humanity posed by Adolf Hitler, they were about to get a very nasty shock.

Right from the outset, the German U Boats had been a deadly threat to shipping, proved by the sinking of the British Liner the SS Athenia on the day that war broke out. The battle for supremacy on the High Seas continued to become more and more desperate, as control of the oceans was vital for all the protagonists. The movement of troops, raw materials and food depended heavily upon shipping and for the people of Britain, an island nation, this was crucial. Although the war ships of the Royal Navy were destroying many enemy craft, they were still being beaten by the might of the German U-Boats.

These submarines could surface and then disappear extremely quickly, speeding through the waters to creep up on ships and destroy them with a barrage of torpedo fire.

Matters for the Allies deteriorated still further when it became clear that things were not going to be much better on land either. Hitler's invasion of Poland, which was the last straw even for those who had supported appeasement, began a campaign that resulted in 70,000 Polish deaths, 133,000 wounded and 700,000 taken prisoner. The German invaders suffered a mere 14,000 casualties and the nation's capital, Warsaw, had no option but to surrender.

The Nazi war machine's new style of warfare, commonly known as Blitzkrieg, or lightning attack, was an unbeatable formula, which continued to become more deadly as they perfected it. Finland was also tied up in a bloody battle with the Russians and although the Fins were fighting bravely, it seemed inevitable that the Red Army of over a million soldiers would inevitably crush the 175,000 strong Finish Army.

However, in Britain, things still seemed relatively quiet. No bombs had fallen on the major cities, troops sat tight awaiting further orders and the Phoney War appeared to be continuing. But for Adolf Hitler it was an extremely busy time and when he issued Fuhrer Directive number six, late in 1939 he was serving notice as to what he intended to do:

An offensive will be planned...through Luxembourg, Belgium and Holland and must be launched at the earliest possible moment...The purpose of this offensive will be to defeat as much as possible of the French army and of the forces of the Allies fighting on their side, and at the same time to win as much territory as possible in Holland, Belgium and northern France to serve as a base for the successful prosecution of the air and sea war against England...

The British Government, still under the control of Prime Minister Neville Chamberlain were reluctant to take the offensive, despite the pleas of Winston Churchill, the First Lord of the Admiralty. Hitler and his Nazi storm troopers had ended 1939 on a high, crushing any attempt at resistance, and if Britain and her Allies didn't act soon, then 1940 would prove to be another great year for Hitler and his New World Order.

The beginning of 1940 saw a big change for the people of Britain that really did show everyone that there was a war on. Rationing was reintroduced on the 8th of January, because many people had already experienced this sharing out of food in the First World War. Nevertheless it still took some getting used to, especially as there were different categories for different types of food. Rationing was however essential for the war effort, Britain had to adjust to consuming less as imports slowed down with German attacks on shipping. The British people were also being encouraged to utilise their gardens to grow food for their families and become self-sufficient, which is where the slogan 'Dig for Victory' originated.

The people of Britain were working together to do all they could, but in contrast it looked as if the government were making little effort to win the war. The first positive action came when it was decided that allied troops would be sent to Finland to help in the fight against the Russians. It was agreed that 100,000 troops would be sent to Finland and as they had to pass through Norway and Sweden to do this, it was hoped the Allies could rally support from these two countries.

However both nations continued to reiterate their neutrality and didn't want to be seen helping the Allies, by allowing them travel through their country. Winston Churchill was one of the politicians trying desperately to get these nations to take to arms against Hitler in the fight for freedom, because he feared that if they did not, then they too would be overrun by the Nazi regime.

The Allies were also discovering just how quick Hitler's Blitz-krieg could be, as the Nazis advanced across Europe. It took far too long for them to mobilize their troops to get to the Fins, because as soon as they were ready in March, the campaign had ended. The Russians had finally broken down the resilient Fin-ish army and forced them to surrender. 25,000 Fins had died in the conflict, yet amazingly the Fins had killed over 200,000 Russian soldiers during the battles. The French leader Daladier had promised the Fins assistance and had failed them with the slowness of his actions. The consequence of this was his own people wanted him out of office as he had been discredited, and on March the 20th 1940, Paul Reynaud replaced Daladier in France.

Despite a large number of Britain's evacuated children return-ing home while all this was going on, due to the apparent lack of danger, the conflict was definitely gathering pace. Food ration-ing was ordered in France, many Canadian pilots and soldiers came to Britain to help with the war effort, Italy served notice that they would fight on the side of the Axis powers and on March the 16th the first British civilian to be killed in an air raid was reported. However, when Hitler announced open warfare at sea, ordering his U-boat commanders to fire on any ship that sailed into British waters; even craft from neutral countries, it soon became evident that there would no longer be a continu-ation of the Phoney War.

Hitler was really stepping up his campaign and more worrying still for the Allies was the fact that he was gaining momentum at incredible speed. Something had to be done and fast. But for the British Government, under the leadership of Prime Minis-ter Neville Chamberlain, again, it was going to be too little, too late. The Allies had decided upon a plan to cut off supplies to Germany, especially Swedish iron-ore, which was crucial to the enemy, shipped out of the Norwegian port of Narvik. The French Prime Minister, Reynaud wanted to seize the port of Narvik so that this could be prevented and in Britain, Winston Churchill was a vociferous supporter of this plan. However, Chamberlain and the war cabinet rejected the idea, although they did allow the Allies to place mines in Norwegian waters.

Winston Churchill had been right about Hitler in 1938, when Chamberlain had talked of appeasement, but no one had listened then, and yet again Churchill's prediction was dismissed until it was proved to be correct, when Hitler turned his attentions towards Norway.

On 7th April 1940, the Nazis began their invasion of Norway and Denmark, taking everyone except Churchill, the First Lord of the Admiralty, by surprise. This attack was a risky venture for Hitler, his troops had to move in quickly before the British Royal Navy had a chance to intercept the ships carrying German tanks and soldiers. Fate was on the side of the Nazis, because the Allies only realised too late what was going on, and when the Germans reached Denmark, the country was totally unprepared, and surrendered almost immediately.

This did give the Norwegian government a warning about the impending invasion, but they still had little time to mobilize their troops. The Germans swiftly took the city of Oslo and a number of major ports and airfields, although elsewhere resistance form the Norwegians was fierce.

The Allies knew they could do nothing to save Denmark and put all their energies into supporting Norway. Between the 10th and 13th of April, ten German destroyers were sunk by British ships while Norway's fleet were also inflicting serious damage on the Nazis. But when Allied troops set foot on Norwegian soil there was no tactical plan, no aerial backup and no supplies being dropped, and despite outnumbering the German invaders, the first Allied offensive was an absolute disaster and they had to retreat from Norway, allowing the Germans to complete their occupation.

Back in Britain the war cabinet were horrified by what had happened, and when news reached the British people, the Prime Minister Neville Chamberlain was blamed once more for not taking a strong enough stand against Adolf Hitler.

Already well past retirement age, Chamberlain knew that the nation no longer had confidence in his leadership, so he chose to resign. Sadly, just six months later Neville Chamberlain died of stomach cancer, aged seventy-one, going down in history as one of Britain's most controversial political leaders. He had done what he had thought was best for Britain, perhaps without grasping just what a threat Hitler really was; something he didn't live long enough to find out.

But the time for considering a negotiated peace had passed with Neville Chamberlain. What Britain and the Allies really needed now was a man of action, and fortunately for all concerned, just such a man was waiting in the wings.

The House of Commons needed a total shake up if they were going to move forward and step up the fight against Hitler, and party politics were put aside when a coalition government was formed. On 10th May, Winston Churchill, who had always understood the threat that Germany's Fuhrer posed, was asked by the King to serve his country as Prime Minister. On his appointment Churchill said that all he could offer was his 'blood, toil, tears and sweat'; however not even he could have predicted just how soon this promise would be put to the test.

On the exact same day of Winston Churchill's appointment and the coalition government was announced, the Nazis invaded

Holland and Belgium. However, this was far more than an extension of Hitler's plans to expand the German empire, it was a carefully planned strategy that required the Allies to come to the aid of Belgium.

The operation, which the German's called Sickle Stroke, was extremely elaborate and could well have crushed the Allied troops.

The evening before the attack Hitler confidently told his staff, *'Gentleman you are about to witness the most famous victory in history!'* The German divisions were split into three groups, the first would invade Belgium and Holland and hopefully draw many Allied troops to the north. Then a second group would attack the Maginot line and keep the Allied troops occupied there, while the third group advanced through the forests of the Ardennes and up through Belgium, to cut off the Allied forces in the north. With the Allies trapped there the other German divisions could attack France with little resistance and quickly snatch power.

The campaign started at 4.30am on the 10th of May with the Luftwaffe bombing Dutch, Belgium, and French airbases, while at the same time ground forces crossed the borders into Belgium and Holland. On the 15th of May, Holland surrendered and just as the Germans had hoped, the Allied troops were sent to Belgium to provide reinforcements. While Western Europe was fighting the war in the north, the real focus of the attack was developing further south. A German Panzer division with 1,800 tanks was edging through the Ardennes Forest without anyone noticing. The Ardennes was virtually undefended as the French thought it could not be penetrated, but the Nazis were proving just how wrong they were.

The situation rapidly deteriorated for the British Expeditionary Force (the BEF) and the Allied forces as the Germans encircled them and pushed them towards the north coast of France. At the same time, the French-Belgium border was being overrun by Nazis, as they pushed west into France at alarming speed.

The Allies were completely surrounded, they couldn't break through the German lines and it was no longer a case of fighting back, but simply a question of survival and the logistics of how to get the Allied soldiers to safety. Hitler increased his strangle hold and pushed thousands of Allied servicemen onto the open beaches of Dunkirk, where they had very little shelter and no protection from German air attacks. Things were looking extremely bleak, and for Winston Churchill just weeks into his premiership, only a miracle would salvage anything from this terrible situation.

Then, to the Allies dismay and delight, Hitler, under council from his staff, ordered the Panzer divisions to halt fifteen miles out of Dunkirk. The German tanks had been the key to this campaign and many either needed maintenance or had broken down, and also the coastal terrain was thought to be unsuitable for the vehicles. That Hitler really wanted to destroy the Allied troops is without question, but he was told that he could afford to wait for backup or leave it for the Luftwaffe to finish the job. The BEF and the Allies had nowhere to run.

With the German tanks no longer advancing, the race was now on to evacuate as many of the Allied troops from Dunkirk as possible, before they were captured or killed. The odds were stacked against the men stranded on the beaches, and had Hitler not ordered his troops to stop when he did, there would have been no possibility of a miracle at Dunkirk. However, Hitler was about to learn a lesson that he would be unwise to forget.

The people of Britain with Winston Churchill running the war effort had an indomitable spirit, and when the Navy requested volunteers with their own craft, whether sailing dinghies, tugboats, or motor cruisers the response was phenomenal. Operation Dynamo was a fearless rescue mission on the part of the British, calling upon the RAF, the Navy and a flotilla of civilian craft to bring the BEF home, to fight another day.

On 27th May, the mass evacuation of Dunkirk commenced, but Hitler was determined to regain the time he had lost, ordering a full scale air and land assault on the thirty-mile stretch of beaches.

The War Office had hoped to be able to save about 50,000 troops from the beaches and as the ships sailed towards Dunkirk, which was lost in black smoke from heavy shelling, even this relatively small number seemed very optimistic. But the battleships and the flotilla of little boats were tireless, some making crossing after crossing to bring the men to safety, while the RAF dominated the skies to keep the relentless attack of the Luftwaffe at bay.

The fates were definitely smiling on the Allies, although the men on the beaches may not have appreciated it at the time. A thick fog swamped the channel for several days, but this helped the ships remain hidden, while keeping many German attack planes grounded.

On the 4th of June as the last boat left for England, an incredible 338,000 Allied soldiers had been rescued, with minimal casualties. This was a truly remarkable achievement for the Allies and a great morale boost for Winston Churchill and the British people.

It was the "Miracle of Dunkirk" and in the dark days ahead, would offer hope when all seemed lost.

Despite the jubilation, Winston Churchill kept the people of Britain focused, commenting that although Dunkirk was a tremendous achievement, wars were not won by evacuations. But when he stood up in the House to give a speech, he inspired the entire nation and served notice on Adolf Hitler, that he now had a fight on his hands.

> *"We shall defend our Island, whatever the costs may be.*
> *We shall fight on the beaches, we shall fight on the landing*
> *grounds, we shall fight in the fields and in the streets, we*
> *shall fight in the hills, we shall never surrender."*

As much of a miracle as the evacuation from Dunkirk was, there is no denying it was still 'a colossal military disaster' that should never have been allowed to happen in the first place. Britain was facing a real threat of an invasion from Germany and even though so many men had been saved, the roads of northern France were littered with Allied vehicles and ordnance.

There has been much speculation about Hitler's judgement call over Dunkirk. Some think he was paving the way for peace talks with Churchill, while others believe he was so focused on reaching Paris, his attention wandered. Nevertheless in the aftermath of the evacuation, his Panzer divisions were storming through the French countryside at alarming speed.

The French were totally unprepared and despite fighting extremely tenaciously, they were no match for Hitler's heavily armoured tank divisions. To the horror of the French, and the rest of the free world, the Nazis marched into Paris on the 14th of June 1940. Hitler had planned to destroy the city, but for today's visitors, thankfully he had a change of heart. So convinced was he by now of his own invincibility, Hitler magnanimously left Paris intact, believing that he would rebuild Berlin to his own design, and outshine Paris and every other city.

To date, Mussolini had kept a fairly low profile, but now the Germans were in the ascendancy, he wanted to share in their glory and on the 10th of June, Italy declared war on France and Britain. Nevertheless, Hitler told Mussolini in no uncertain terms to stay out of France until it was controlled by Germany, as this was to be an all-German victory. Britain tried to organise an Anglo-French union on the 16th of June, but it was too late and even Prime Minister Reynaud resigned, leaving the newly appointed Marshal Petain with no option but to surrender.

Just a few days later on the 21st of June, at Rethonedes near Compiegne, French representatives signed an armistice to end the fighting. It was perhaps no coincidence that the place where this armistice was signed was the exact same spot where the German armistice of 1918 was signed. Hitler always thought his country was humiliated by the original armistice which ended World War I, and it appeared that he was finally getting revenge for the humiliation. The terms of the armistice were clear, Petain's government would remain sovereign, but Northern and Western France were to become German occupation zones and Italy would be permitted to occupy areas of southern France.

The French would even have to pay for the Germans occupation costs, while two million French prisoners would remain in German hands. Hitler wanted to totally humiliate the French with this armistice, giving no compromises. Hitler believed that this is exactly what happened to Germany in 1918, and just 22 years later, he took his revenge.

The short campaign between May the 10th and June the 22nd had been a complete success for Germany, bringing them control of France, Belgium, and Holland, while pushing the BEF out of mainland Europe. The Nazis lost only 27,000 soldiers to achieve this, in contrast to the 120,000 lost by the French.

So far, Hitler had relied on the strength of his Panzer divisions to win his battles, reinforced by the Luftwaffe. But as he turned his attention to his invasion plans for Great Britain a change of tactics was going to be called for. Despite the difficulties faced by the British, being surrounded by waters that were blockaded by German U Boats, there was a distinct advantage in being cut off from mainland Europe, as the tanks would need to be transported to take the battle to Britain.

Hitler had little respect for France and believed they would be crushed with relative ease. However, he was not so confident about Britain, because he knew the British forces, under Churchill's leadership, would be tough to overcome. Consequently Hitler once again tried to extend his hand in peace to Churchill, asking that Britain recognise Nazi supremacy in Europe.

By this stage Hitler was already planning to break his non-aggression pact with Stalin and invade Russia, which he knew would put great demands on his resources. But he also knew Winston Churchill of old and must have realised there would be no capitulation by the British. Consequently Operation Sealion was drawn up for the invasion of Britain and Winston Churchill prepared his people for the trials and tribulations that lay ahead. He announced that he believed the battle of Britain would start very soon and everyone had a part to play and needed to be ready. So far civilian casualties had been minimal, but that was all about to change, and there were some very tough decisions to be taken.

The responsibility of leadership for Churchill required him to take swift action after the fall of Paris, and on the 3rd of July Churchill ordered the destruction of the French fleet at Mers-el-Kebir in North Africa. Although technically the fleet was still under French control, Churchill feared that Hitler might well seize the ships, to strengthen any attack on the British Navy.

Tragically 1,250 French sailors were killed in the mission, which took just five minutes to complete. The French were furious at what they viewed to be an unprovoked raid, but in

Britain the attack, although causing many innocent deaths, was regarded as a necessary tactical manoeuvre. Even the American President, Franklin D Roosevelt applauded Churchill's brave move, and when Germany declared that Article 8 of the French armistice would be suspended, Churchill was completely vindicated.

This basically meant that the Germans would have been able to commandeer the French Navy to increase their own, but Churchill's quick reactions prevented this from happening, leaving Hitler with the demanding task of overcoming the Royal Navy if Operation Sealion was to stand any chance of succeeding.

On the home front, the British were gearing up to resist any German invasion with the war effort ranging from collecting scrap steel to over a million men joining the Home Guard. The women of Britain were encouraged to work in the factories, as well as looking after their families, and production of aircraft like the Spitfire and the Hurricane went into overdrive.

Other women went to work on farms as land army girls, replacing the men who had gone to war, to ensure a constant supply of food for the nation. Barrage balloons were hoisted up all around the major cities to prevent enemy planes from flying in too low, catching them in the strong wire and destroying them if they did. If Hitler was coming to invade Britain, the British would be ready for him and whether mending and making do, digging for victory or cooking up nutritious meals from the fields and hedgerows, the spirit of the people was as indomitable as it had been at Dunkirk.

The Royal Navy was the first big problem for Hitler, when it came to the invasion of Britain, because the German Navy, without the addition of the French ships destroyed at Mers-el-Kebir, was definitely inferior. However, the Luftwaffe was on paper at least, much stronger than the RAF so Hitler believed that by using his aircraft to destroy the British planes and airbases, he would then be able to attack the Royal Navy without hindrance from the air.

Basically, whoever had control of the skies would be able to control Britain and Hitler believed, like all his conquests to date, victory was a forgone conclusion. But, yet again he failed to add the British spirit of determination, inspired by the leadership of Winston Churchill, into the equation, and just as it had at Dunkirk, it was an error of judgement that would cost him dear.

The Battle of Britain began on 10th July 1940, and from the outset the Germans were confident that they could quickly destroy the RAF as they outnumbered them in terms of both planes and trained pilots. Interestingly after Dunkirk, the press had played down the important role played by the RAF in the rescue, and there was a quiet confidence amongst the pilots and the commanders, especially as they knew that increased factory production meant that over 200 planes a month were being constructed.

The British also had the distinct advantage of fighting on home territory, as the Germans had a much greater distance to travel before engaging the enemy, and fuel capacity was a major issue. What's more, the British could also detect the incoming planes with a revolutionary new system called RADAR.

Both the British and the Germans had been involved with the development of radio waves, although just before the outbreak of war the British Air Ministry were concerned that the Germans were using this technology to develop a "death ray". They approached radio researcher Robert Watson-Watt for verification, but he assured them that this was unlikely and pointed them towards Radio Detection and Ranging, which we all know today as RADAR, for plotting enemy positions.

Consequently at the start of World War II a number of RADAR stations known as Chain Home were constructed along the south and east coast of England, and by 1940 as the Battle of Britain loomed large, the RAF were already in possession of a powerful weapon that the Luftwaffe failed to appreciate the significance of.

On the 1st of August Hitler sent out the order, which demanded that the Luftwaffe "overpower the English air force with all the forces at its command in the shortest possible time". The targets for the Germans were planes, airbases, and aircraft factories, because to achieve Hitler's objective the RAF had to be taken out at every level. Hordes of German *(pronounced M E not me)* Me109 and Me100 planes were sent to fight the British in the skies over the South East of England.

As soon as the RADAR system picked up the presence of the incoming planes the RAF would take to the air to meet with them in the clouds. Although the Spitfire was slightly superior to the German fighters, the pilots still had to rely on their skills and wit to escape bullet fire and take the enemy down. Many people on the ground looked upwards during the summer and autumn of 1940 to see the skies littered with the desperate dogfights.

Losses were heavy on both sides and there was no indication of who was gaining the upper hand. The Luftwaffe kept sending fighters over to Britain and the RAF kept utilising the RADAR system to go and meet them. Bombers were also being sent over from Germany to destroy the airfields and in the south of England the bases suffered serious damage as a result of this. The bravery of the RAF Pilots was really starting to make a significant difference, as typified in this account of a skirmish with the Luftwaffe.

I was forced to retire owing to engine failure but dived on a Ju87.
After a three second burst it went into an inverted dive straight into
the sea. My engine started again so I went after another Ju87 and
attacked him before he was able to dive bomb the convoy. He dived
into the sea at high speed. After this my engine packed up for good.

Fortunately, the pilot did manage to get back safely after this and he flew again the next day, determined that the Germans would never be victorious. Many more tales of courage and valour can be found from this period and without the bravery of these young fighter pilots, the outcome of the Battle of Britain would have been very different indeed.

In fact at the height of the skirmishes on 20th August 1940, Winston Churchill stood up in the House of Commons and delivered the ultimate tribute to the RAF, saying, *"Never in the field of human conflict was so much owed by so many to so few".*

British newspapers were reporting the plane losses like football match scores, some days the Luftwaffe won and other days the RAF. Pilots were being sent from all over the world to help the RAF from Canada, New Zealand, India, and South Africa. Even though the Americans were yet to enter the war, there were also US Air Force pilots who volunteered to fly for the Allies.

The RADAR system was also proving to be of major importance. The Chain Home stations could estimate how many enemy planes were incoming, how far away they were and at what altitude. Although the Luftwaffe made a series of small raids on the RADAR stations early on in the operation, the British restored them within a few days. Also RADAR like signals were broadcast from other locations to cause confusion and eventually the Germans stopped trying to bomb them, evidently unaware of just how vital the system was to the RAF.

The battle continued into the autumn and for two weeks between the 24th of August and the 6th of September, the RAF lost 290 fighter aircraft, while the Luftwaffe lost 380. However, for the Germans over half of these losses were bombers, while it was the fighter planes and pilots that were essential to winning this particular battle, and with the RAF now facing serious pilot shortages, it looked as if defeat was just days away for the British. Then, just as had happened at Dunkirk, a change of tactic by the Germans opened a window of opportunity.

The Luftwaffe pilots were ordered to stop bombing the ports and airfields of southern England and to move inland and start bombing Britain's cities. With the benefit of hindsight, historians view this as a significant error of judgement because with the Luftwaffe heading further inland the RAF had longer to marshal their interception, while the southern airfields were allowed a much-needed period of respite to repair and replenish.

One of the major reasons for this change of tactics was Hitler's desire to target Britain's cities in revenge for air raids on German cities, but this was all the result of a misunderstanding. A German plane being pursued by an RAF fighter, dropped its bombs over London and Winston Churchill, believing that this was a deliberate action, retaliated, sending British bombers to Germany.

From the 7th of September onwards the Luftwaffe headed for England to bomb London. Hitler was furious about the Allied attacks and was determined to destroy Britain's cities, and many believe that this cold-blooded need for revenge distracted the Fuhrer and helped the RAF to recover.

They were just as busy in the air, but when they landed, they could rest without fear of bombing, and they took advantage of the situation to repair their equipment and runways.

Hitler continued to step up his bombing raids and the Blitz, as it was known, became a time of terror for the British. On 15th September, the Luftwaffe sent their biggest fleet yet. With 200 bombers and a vast fighter escort, Hitler wanted to bomb London into the ground. The RAF threw all that they had at the attack and destroyed 60 of the bombers, serving notice to the Germans that they were far from being a spent force.

When Hitler began Operation Sealion it was summer and he truly believed he would be victorious before the onset of winter, but without even completing phase one, his plans would have to change. Trying to invade Britain had become too costly, he was losing too many aircraft, his naval fleet was still being repaired and the tides would not be right for a sea attack until the spring. Also Hitler was beginning to look seriously eastwards, planning his invasion of Russia and he needed to keep as much in reserve as possible for this major undertaking.

On 17th September Hitler announced the postponement of Operation Sealion; the battle for Britain had been won, at least for the time being. The brave pilots of the RAF and the tactics of ground control with their revolutionary RADAR system had saved the nation from invasion, and after just a matter of months in the office of Prime Minister, Winston Churchill had prevented Hitler from achieving a military goal.

Nevertheless, the bombing didn't stop with the threat of invasion lessening. Germany continued to bomb the nation's major cities and London, Cardiff, Manchester, Coventry, Southampton, and Liverpool all came under fire. Thousands of bombs rained down on the people during the night-time raids. Hitler hoped that this would not only crush the major industrial sites, but also destroy the nation's moral as well. Evidently, he at last realised that the British wartime spirit was a force to be reckoned with.

At the same time the German U-boats were targeting the many

ships bound for Britain carrying vital supplies. If the Nazis could not take Britain, then maybe they could starve the nation into submission by cutting off food and resources, effectively keeping the British out of the rest of the war. Also the bombings continued through 1940 and well into 1941, but rather than achieving Hitler's aim, the attacks helped to unite the people of Britain even more, and as the raids got worse, the levels of public determination to beat the Nazis simply grew and grew.

But the war was not just being fought in the skies above Britain, further action was being taken all over the world. The Japanese had been fighting their own battles in the Far East, intent on being the superpower in Asia, but officially joined Hitler's Axis powers on the 27th of September. It was agreed that the Japanese would recognise the new German-Italian authority in Europe and likewise the Germans and Italians would recognise Japan's power in Asia. It was also agreed that if any of them were attacked by a power not involved in the European war, then the others would come to their aid.

This was of course directly aimed at the United States of America, a major threat to Hitler in Europe if they entered the war on the side of the Allies, while constantly watching the activities of the Japanese in the Pacific.

Despite the fact that the Americans did not want to fight a war on foreign soil, President Roosevelt had an excellent relationship with Winston Churchill and the British and was helping the Allies significantly. The USA had recently swapped 50 war ships for a 99-year lease of British Naval and air bases in the western hemisphere, and looking ahead, on the 16th of September, Roosevelt introduced conscription. Now all Americans between the ages of 21 and 35 could be drafted for Military service. Although it would be more than a year before America would suffer a direct attack from the Axis powers, President Roosevelt was already preparing for what was to come.

Elsewhere the Italians were really beginning to step up their war campaign. They had already taken parts of British Somaliland, in the Horn of Africa, during the summer months and were now invading Greece. On October the 28th Mussolini marched his troops into Greece with the jubilant cry of *"Fuhrer, we are on the march".*

Hitler however was furious at Mussolini's actions, viewing this as a tactical debacle. The Italian troops were not ready for war, but Mussolini was inspired by Hitler's success and was determined to emulate it in the Mediterranean. As Hitler expected, the Italians suffered a humiliating defeat at the hands of the Greeks, and on the 21st of November the Italians fled the country.

The world was now definitely at war and as 1940 drew to a close, London experienced the full power of Hitler's Luftwaffe when over 22,000 firebombs were dropped on the capital on the 30th of December. It was a chilling end to the year, as Britain fought on alone, with Hitler's Axis powers growing stronger daily. These were dark times for Britain and the rest of the democratic world, and as thoughts turned to what 1941 would bring, any hopes of peace on earth and good will to men seemed futile, while Hitler's reign of terror continued.

WORLD WAR II HISTORY JOURNALS: 1941

There were no church bells to ring in the New Year of 1941. The people of Britain knew that if the bells rang it would be to warn them of a German invasion, so for the duration of the war, whatever the occasion, the church bells remained silent.

This was a time when the threat of invasion was at its worst, despite the miracle of deliverance at Dunkirk, some six months earlier, when more than 300,000 Allied service men were rescued from the beaches of northern France by a flotilla of civilian craft and the Royal Navy. If the RAF had not won the Battle of Britain in the autumn of 1940, in the skies over England's green and pleasant land, the Nazis would have already been staking a claim to British soil. However, in practice, the RAF's remarkable achievement proved to be a reprieve rather than a decisive victory, as the British faced a New Year of terrible uncertainty with Hitler looking to expand the German Empire still further, across the English Channel.

Although Britain had to date managed to withstand a sustained German onslaught, many of her Allies had not, and to make matters worse the Axis powers were gaining strength all the time. When Japan, Germany and Italy signed their tripartite pact, before bringing in Hungary, Romania, and Slovakia towards the end of 1940, it looked as if their rise to supremacy could not be stopped.

German bombers were devastating Britain's major cities and while the nation's wartime spirit was riding high, the Blitz really was taking its toll. But despite Hitler being kept from the British mainland, out at sea the Germans were winning a very important battle.

Hitler had increased the German U-boat fleet and the plan of action was to try and starve the British into surrender. The U-boats were able to effectively control sea routes to the United Kingdom and were successfully destroying many thousands of tons of essential supplies and shipping on a regular basis. Britain relied heavily upon the import of goods and throughout 1941 the government, under the leadership of Prime Minister Winston Churchill, found it increasingly difficult to keep the supply line intact.

With all Britain's neighbouring Allies under German occupation, it was difficult for Winston Churchill to go on the offensive, as he needed to constantly watch the nation's defences. Nevertheless the RAF had been engaged in bombing raids on German cities while the Luftwaffe continued their nightly raids. Hitler believed the British people would demand their government surrender to Germany, and the attacks were well planned and sustained.

Sadly the RAF bombing raids were far less organised, and the number of airmen lost were equal to the German casualties they inflicted. Winston Churchill's promise that there would be no surrender still stood firm, but in the early days of 1941, any assistance, especially from America, would be very gratefully received.

However, if anyone had said at this stage in the proceedings that before the year was out, Hitler's own errors of judgement would actually help the Allied cause, few would have believed them. But such were the twists and turns of fate in 1941 that this would indeed prove to be the case.

In the build up to World War II there were many Americans who adopted an isolationist policy, but fortunately for the free world, Franklin D Roosevelt who had been President since

1933, recognised the threat that Adolf Hitler posed and did everything he could to help the war effort, short of entering the conflict to fight on the side of the Allies. Roosevelt undoubtedly enjoyed an excellent relationship with Winston Churchill, and when he delivered his State of the Union Address on 6th January, the British Prime Minister must have been greatly encouraged.

The speech, alternatively known as the "Four Freedoms" insisted that human beings everywhere in the world had a right to Freedom of speech and expression, Freedom to worship, Freedom from want, and Freedom from fear. That Adolf Hitler was denying these basic human rights as he stormed his way through Europe was now evident, and Roosevelt served notice of his commitment to the Allies, saying that America should support any cause that fought for the "Four Freedoms".

He also declared that America, rather than lend money to Britain, should supply arms that could be paid for after the war was won. Consequently on 10th January he introduced "Lend-Lease" to Congress, but there were still those who believed a peaceful settlement to the growing global conflict could be found.

With powerful pressure groups like the "America First Committee" vehemently opposing intervention, Roosevelt would have to convince his countrymen that the time for action had come, and it was far from being an easy task. Even the great American aviator Charles Lindbergh, a national hero who was famous for making the first solo, non-stop flight across the Atlantic, testified before congress on 23rd January, his belief that the USA should negotiate a neutrality pact with Hitler. So for the time being at least Winston Churchill and the people of Britain would have to continue the fight for freedom in Europe, without American intervention.

While seemingly standing alone in Europe, the British were also making progress with the BEF (the British Expeditionary Force), who were hard at work fighting off the Italians in Africa. Much of the nation's war effort was being channelled in this direction because the armed forces were still far from ready for an offensive in Europe, so they concentrated on keeping Mussolini's army contained on the neighbouring continent.

In fact the Allies were doing such a good job at pushing back the Italians, that on the 19th of January Mussolini had to humbly apply to Hitler for more troops to help out. Hitler was more than happy to oblige, but only on the proviso that Mussolini agreed to total subordination in all military matters in the future.

Meanwhile back on the home front, the British were still under attack from the Luftwaffe's constant bombing raids as Hitler continued his campaign to break the nation's spirit. Many of Britain's major cities were ablaze night after night, and there were so many fires that some buildings just had to be left to burn.

There was no doubt that what the civilian population faced should have by rights been beyond endurance, but somehow everyone pulled together. There was no discrimination between rich and poor, the bombs landed on Buckingham Palace and the slums of Whitechapel, and King George VI and Queen Elizabeth walked amongst their fellow Londoners to share their losses, offer their condolences, and help the people to keep their spirits up. In underground shelters folk shared what they had, looked after frightened children, and sang together the popular songs of the time while the bombs exploded around them. By morning as they surfaced to assess the damage, the lucky whose homes remained intact, helped those less fortunate before going to work, keeping the nation going and the war effort alive.

The Blitz continued through February, and although the people of Britain couldn't possibly have realised it, their tenacity and never say die attitude was actually paying dividends. On 6th February, Hitler's war directive number 23, titled 'Directions for Operations against the English War Economy' stated that the Luftwaffe's night-time activities had:

> *Least effect of all, so far as we can see, on morale and the will to resist of the English people. No decisive success can be expected from terror attacks on residential areas.*

The British people had shown the Nazis that no matter what was thrown at them they would, just as Winston Churchill had promised, never surrender.

With this in mind, Hitler decided to change tactics and further increase his attacks on British ports and shipping. This campaign had been very successful so far as it had stopped many vital supplies from getting into Britain. This was very important for another reason too, providing a smoke screen for what Hitler was really planning as his next move.

It was only the Germans that knew they were not going to attempt an invasion of Great Britain at this point in the conflict. For the rest of the world Operation Sealion, the German code name for the invasion, was as much of a threat as ever and by continuing to keep up the bombing raids Hitler simply perpetuated the idea. Everyone believed that this was the focus of Hitler's empire building strategy and for the cities suffering the nightly onslaughts, there seemed to be no end to the misery.

By stepping up his attacks on British ports and out at sea Hitler gave Winston Churchill and the government the impression that the invasion was imminent. In reality Hitler, even in the early weeks of 1941, had no intention whatsoever of doing this, but keeping as many British troops on home territory as possible would prevent any possible disruption of Hitler's next invasion plan, code named Operation Barbarossa, that would target Russia.

The non-aggression pact between Hitler and Stalin, agreed just before the Nazis marched into Poland in 1939, triggering Chamberlain's declaration of war against Germany, had come as a surprise for the rest of the world because of the two leader's mutual hostility, and throughout the early skirmishes of the war, they viewed each other with great suspicion.

Many believe that Hitler never intended to keep to the pact and was simply stopping Stalin being a problem until he had the power to invade, and by 1941 he had Russia in his sights, and Operation Barbarossa was ready for implementation.

In Hitler's "Mein Kampf" written while he was in prison in 1924 before his rise to power, he made it clear that the German people needed Lebensraum, which translates as living space. For land to do this he looked to the east and declared it was Nazi party policy to kill, deport, or enslave Russian and other Slavic populations, many of whom were Jews. So the warnings of what was to come were there for all to see, long before Hitler was in a position to carry out what he threatened. But now he believed he was invincible, and it was time to rekindle old grievances.

To Hitler, destroying the Soviet Union would benefit his Aryan master race for generations to come, providing slave labour and raw materials for the German industry, cheap food for his people and precious fuel from the Russian Oilfields. He also believed this would isolate Britain still further, and Churchill, in his view, would have no choice but to surrender once Russia had fallen.

The Nazi pre-occupation with racial hygiene, basically geno-
cide, was driven by Hitler's anti-Semitic view, and throughout
1941 the campaign against the Jewish people became increasingly brutal.

More and more Jews were being transported to the dreaded concentration camps and those who escaped this terrible fate were
left to try and survive in the ghettos.

Jewish families were rounded up and forced to live in horrendous conditions and surviving in the ghetto was equally as
tough as it was in the concentration camps. On 31st January,
in the Warsaw ghetto alone it was reported that sixty-five Jews
were dying of starvation every day. The governor, Hans Frank
had a calculated policy which made sure only half the food that
was needed was made available to the ghetto. Consequently the
starving masses would do anything for the promise of more
food, and this ensured that they always followed orders. Frank
coldly claimed:

*Killing a Jew by hunger saves a valuable bullet, needed for
the master race's inevitable conquest of the world*

And matters were about to get much worse for the Jewish
people as the Nazis started their first experiments using gas
chambers, for their mass extermination programmes in the
Concentration Camps. Not that the Jews were alone in their
suffering; homosexuals, ethnic minorities, freemasons, the dis-
abled and the elderly were all systematically targeted and it
would be another year before the rest of the world truly learnt
of the evil depths Adolf Hitler and his Nazis were capable of
sinking to.

While Hitler was busy planning his foray into Russia, the Italian
army under Mussolini were running into stiff opposition from

the Allies. In Africa alone in two short months, the Italians had lost 130,000 soldiers as prisoners of war, 380 tanks and 845 guns. On February the 14th Hitler had to send the first wave of his 'Afrika Korps' to help in the battle against the British.

Field Marshall Erwin Rommel, the German commander known as the Desert Fox, had also been promised additional armoured divisions but as a result of Mussolini's incompetence, these could not to be sent before April, and until then Rommel was expected just to hold ground. But he wasn't called the Desert Fox for nothing. He wanted to attack the British using hoax tanks. These would be dummy vehicle bodies mounted onto Volkswagen engines and as absurd as it may sound, it was a workable idea because Volkswagen engines powered some of Germany's most successful military vehicles, like the Kubelwagen and Schwimmagen.

Several years earlier in 1934, Adolf Hitler had commissioned Ferdinand Porsche to produce the first people's car, otherwise known as the Volkswagen. Hitler wanted a cheap reliable family car that was affordable to the people of Germany. Just as the first KDF Wagen was ready to come rolling of the production line war broke out and civilian car production was halted. However, Porsche being the clever designer he was, took the blueprints of this exceptionally resilient vehicle and adapted them for military requirements. So these fake tanks with their Volkswagen machinery couldn't have been more authentic, especially as they had a revolutionary air-cooled engine that proved invaluable in the heat of Africa.

Despite the progress being made against the Italians, and their German reinforcements, February proved to be one of the worst months for Allied shipping. The German U boats were sinking many merchant craft, the Luftwaffe were consistently scoring more direct hits on shipping and Hitler's new acoustic mines that were detonated by the sound of a ship were inflicting terrible casualties.

The British were really struggling, with the last U-boat hit being the U104, destroyed before Christmas 1940, and in fact the Germans had lost only thirty-two submarines, since the outbreak of the war.

To make matters worse the Axis powers were gaining ground at an alarming rate. Romania allowed Germany to use the country as a base to attack neighbouring Bulgaria, Yugoslavia, and Greece.

Quickly the Germans took Bulgaria, with little resistance and the beleaguered nation joined the Axis Powers on the 1st of March. Days later Hitler put further pressure on Yugoslavia and the situation in the Balkans became very worrying indeed for the Allies.

The British knew how grave the situation was as the Nazis were now poised to take their Greek Allies as well. Winston Churchill was in desperate need of help and on the 11th of March relief finally seemed to be getting through. President Roosevelt signed into law the "lend-lease" bill that he'd promised in January. This bill effectively made the United States a partner of Britain in the war, making America, as one politician described it, "an arsenal for the democracies, seeking to carry out Roosevelt's pledge to send to these countries in ever-increasing numbers, ships, aeroplanes, tanks and guns.

Assistance could not have come at a better moment for the British, it was estimated that the war was costing eleven million pounds a day and the economy was getting to the point where it could no longer support the conflict.

Economically however, since the Luftwaffe had spread the bombing raids wider, the intensive spending on wreckage clearances and repairs, that had been seen when London alone the focus of the Blitz, had subsided a little.

And then, just when a glimmer of hope appeared on the horizon, the people of Britain were taken completely by surprise, when on the 8th of March new bombing initiatives began over much of the nation. Many believed that Hitler had been saving his aircraft for use elsewhere, but now some of the largest attack forces since the Blitz began, were now being reported. 244 bombers were sent over Portsmouth on the 11th of March, killing 750 citizens in two nights of intense air raids. Cardiff, London, Manchester, and Birmingham were all targeted again by these relentless Luftwaffe onslaughts. Burning buildings were lighting up the night sky once more, and try as the fire-fighters might, to extinguish the flames, the bombs just kept on coming.

Night after night the intensity of the raids increased and on the night of the 16th of March, 122,292 incendiaries were dropped on London by what was reported to have been several hundred planes. Everyone was yet again on heightened alert, expecting a Nazi invasion any day. The smoke screen was doing its job.

Hitler was indeed on the move elsewhere, on the 27th of March he ordered his troops to smash Yugoslavia into submission. There was a popular uprising against the Nazis as the ordinary people stormed the streets shouting, "Long live Britain" and "down with Hitler". But what of the German response?

The Nazis stormed through Yugoslavia, continuing to brutally kill civilians, long after the battle was won. After 12 days of intense fighting Yugoslavia surrendered to the Nazis, Hitler's Blitzkrieg once again reigned supreme, and the Germans immediately invaded Greece, just as the British had feared they would.

The Nazis were, for the time being at least, unstoppable. The bombs kept falling on Britain and the tanks kept rolling through the Balkans. In May, Liverpool was bombed for seven consecutive nights, killing thousands of people, and destroying hundreds of homes, while Rommel's desert fighters were forcing the Allies into retreat in Africa.

But it wasn't quite all doom and gloom. On the 9th of May Allied forces boarded a German U-Boat. Although positive, it was nothing out of the ordinary, but what they recovered onboard was. The British were able to retrieve an intact Enigma cipher machine with codebooks. This was immediately sent to Bletchley Park in Milton Keynes, where the wartime code breakers were based and they set to work, solving this particular Enigma in record time. The Experts worked night and day at Bletchley and when they cracked the code it was possible for military intelligence to decipher German transmissions, and at last they could predict where the lethal U-boats would strike next.

The cracking of the Enigma code didn't come a moment too soon, with Hitler and his growing Axis powers completely dominating the conflict, and he continued to pile on the pressure. On the 11th of May in the region of 500 German bombers flew over London delivering their most deadly attack to date.

Eyewitnesses reported that by morning all that could be seen along the skyline of the Capital was a mass of black smoke as hundreds of fires still burned. The trains couldn't run, a third of the streets were impassable due to rubble, 150,000 people were left without power, or water and 5,000 homes were completely destroyed. The Blitz, far from easing, had reached a new level of horror. Britain was trying her hardest to fight back with barrage balloons and anti-aircraft guns, but the guns were rarely accurate, and the balloons could only stop low flying aircraft.

Every day seemed to be filled with more bad news for the Allies and on the 24th of May the British battle cruiser, HMS Hood, was sunk by the German battleship, the Bismarck, killing all but three of the 1,416 strong crew. Just days later the Bismarck was sunk in the North Atlantic by the Allies but any hope of stopping Hitler was slipping away from them. In the same week hordes of German paratroopers landed on the Island of Crete and although the Allies knew that the paratroopers were coming, thanks to the cracking of Enigma, they were simply unprepared for the bombings and the sheer number of troops.

On the 1st of June, just a week after the Germans had landed on Crete the British had no choice but to withdraw, despite putting up a brave fight. Then two weeks later the Germans pushed the Allies back over the Libyan-Egyptian border in what had been meant to be a major British counter-offensive to relieve the siege of Tobruk. Churchill had great hopes for this operation, code named Battle-axe, but sadly after losing 91 tanks to the Germans 25, the Allies were defeated yet again.

The Year was almost halfway through and power was once again sliding to the Axis. The Allies had very few successful missions, many British cities lay in ruins and the unstoppable German Panzer divisions seemed to be able to crush everything in their path. Apart from a few pockets of resistance, the Axis controlled much of Europe and whenever the British tried to counter-attack they were swiftly beaten back.

The Allies needed a miracle if they were to even entertain the idea of victory and apart from the rescue at Dunkirk, almost a year ago to the day, miracles seemed to be in pretty short supply. But just like had happened at Dunkirk, when the Germans lost focus in their haste to get to Paris, Hitler was looking beyond Europe and North Africa to begin his biggest offensive manoeuvre of the war.

On the 22nd of June at 3.15am Hitler set Operation Barbarossa in motion. Over 3 million German troops, 3,600 tanks and 2,700 aircraft crossed the Russo-German border as the Nazis attacked Russia. Although always suspicious of Hitler the Russians could not believe what was happening. The Soviet generals were even warned of Operation Barbarossa, thanks to accurate undercover intelligence, some weeks prior to the German invasion, but they considered the notion preposterous.

And if the Russians were surprised, just imagine the shock for the British, who had been expecting an invasion any day. With cities lying in ruins and the recent escalation of bombing raids, the people and the government were anticipating Hitler would finish what he had started.

Stalin, although concerned by Hitler's activities in the Balkans, still believed that the huge expanse of the Soviet Union would be too big an area for the Nazis to dominate. He also felt confident that he would be able to negotiate a settlement with Hitler. The day after the German invasion, Hungary and Slovakia declared war on Russia, followed by Finland on the 26th of June and Albania on the 28th.

Hitler was undaunted at the prospect of taking on the mighty Red Army because he was by now sure he was invincible. His belief in Aryan racial purity grew more and more obsessive and he was convinced the Russian people were inferior beings. The German dictator had set out his intentions months earlier, making it clear that he had no respect for the Russians or their Bolshevik leader:

> *The war against Russia will be such that it cannot be conducted in a knightly fashion; the struggle is one of ideologies and racial differences and will have to be conducted with unprecedented, unmerciful, and unrelenting harshness.*

When it was evident the Russians were at war with Germany, Churchill, being the shrewd politician he was, told Stalin that

Britain would supply any technical and economic assistance that they could, so together they could stand firm against Hitler. Whatever had happened previously was put aside, Russia was now fighting on the side of the Allies and if Hitler underestimated the Soviets, he did so at his peril, and as this statement from him proves, he truly believed the Russian campaign a forgone conclusion:

We have only to kick in the door and the whole rotten structure will come crashing down.

Hitler predicted that Russia would be crushed in less than four months, and targeting the cities of Leningrad, Moscow and Kiev, the attacks appeared to be on course. In the first week of fighting they had taken 150,000 prisoners and destroyed 1,200 Russian tanks. The Luftwaffe was also winning the battle in the sky against the Red Air Force, but the Russians fought back courageously on every front.

Stalin ordered a scorched earth policy, to stop the German tanks, which entailed the people of Russia destroying their own homes, ruining their crops, and burning any fuel so there would be nothing left to run the Nazi war machine. Another invader, the French Emperor Napoleon had also underestimated the Russians many years before Hitler, and it was an error of judgement that cost him dear. The scorched earth tactic had worked against Napoleon in the early 19th Century, and Stalin was confident it would work again.

Even so the Germans were extremely successful in their offensive, pushing the Russians back towards Moscow. The Nazi treatment of prisoners was brutal, with many thousands being massacred, but this actually worked in the Russians' favour. If they surrendered, they would be slaughtered, so the Soviets had nothing to lose and everything to fight for, and they certainly did.

Also, the Russian climate began to play its part as the autumn rains came early and turned the Soviet roads into quagmires. In a very short time the weather was hindering Hitler's tanks and they could only operate at 35% efficiency, while the winter snows were yet to come. But Hitler was determined to push on, believing he could still crush Russian resistance before the year was out.

For Hitler, the eradication of inferior races was fast becoming an obsession. He ordered that all Jews would now have to wear yellow stars so they could be recognised, and on the 3rd of September at Auschwitz the first experiments using the gas chambers were carried out. 600 Russian prisoners of war and 250 Jews were squeezed into a tiny cellar where a powder was thrown into the room, which let off a deadly gas, killing them all. Hitler now had the means to step up his campaign of ethnic cleansing.

Back in Russia, although the weather was helping the Red Army, the Germans were still making advances. By early October they were only 50 miles away from the centre of Moscow, and things were beginning to look bleak for the Red Army. That was until a Russian spy in the Far East discovered that Japan had no intention of attacking Russia in the future as Germany's ally, as they were concentrating all their efforts in the Pacific. With no fear of a Japanese attack from the east Stalin could mobilise his Eastern divisions and bring them into Moscow to keep the Germans at bay.

The battle for Russia was going to be long and bloody and would not be concluded as Hitler had hoped in 1941.

October turned to November and the fighting continued, while the weather turned more severe. At least 100,000 German soldiers got frostbite in the winter of 1941 and there were 2,000 amputations as a result. The Nazis were simply not prepared for the winter, wearing very light clothing, compared to the well-insulated uniforms of the Red Army. In December Hitler even tried to call off all offensives until the spring, because of the dreadful weather and the severe losses they were suffering, which many of his generals supported.

But Hitler was becoming ever more erratic in his decision making and was determined not to suffer a defeat as Napoleon had, after retreating from Moscow, and he changed his mind at the last minute. On the 16th of December he announced that there would be no withdrawal of troops and the fighting must go on. Many of Hitler's high commanders believed this to be suicide, but no one dared argue with the Fuhrer.

Now, while the Germans struggled on thorough the Russian winter, tensions were definitely mounting in the Pacific. 1941 had seen Japan consistently and confidently expand their empire in the Far East and America was getting increasingly concerned about what was happening so close to home. The United States had always been a major power in the Pacific, and it appeared that the Japanese were getting ready to challenge this.

By the end of the 1930s, Japan had become extensively militarised, including a huge modern Navy and as they escalated the conflict with China, in the Second Sin-Japanese War, Japan had no choice but resign from the League of Nations. America at this time showed its disapproval by terminating its commercial treaty with Japan.

The impact of this became clear when the US put an embargo on scrap metal and gasoline shipments to Japan, followed by a complete oil embargo early in 1941. Japan's lack of any oil of its own gave the growing Axis power a real difficulty. 80% of Japan's oil had been supplied by America and they looked around for an alternative source, with a view to possibly seizing the Dutch East Indies. However one thing was absolutely for certain, any such act of aggression would immediately bring America into the war.

So the Japanese were well aware that they could not control the Far East completely unless they could supply all of their own raw materials, especially oil, and the prospect of going to war with America was therefore going to have to be seriously considered. Nevertheless the Americans were a military force to be reckoned with, and the Japanese commanders were without doubt sharp military strategists. They realised that if they were to stand any chance of victory over the USA, they would have to strike first, with the element of surprise. What's more they would have to strike decisively, to totally devastate the United States in the Pacific, and the Japanese plans to destroy the American Fleet began to take shape way back in 1940.

Fleet Admiral Isoroku Yamamoto first requested Naval Intelligence on Pearl Harbour, Hawaii in February 1940 and by the spring of 1941 he'd had spies put in place. The idea of a pre-emptive strike on the American Fleet gained momentum as sketches of the Naval base were gathered almost daily by the spy, Takeo Yoshikawa, and when he discovered that Sunday was the day when the most ships would be in the harbour, the plans really started to take shape.

Through the summer of 1941 the Japanese pilots trained in the skies over the Island of Kyushu with Major General Minoru Genda planning the attack. His strategy was very clear, as was his intent:

"In the event of outbreak of war with the United States, there would be little prospect of our operations succeeding unless, at

*the very outset, we can deal a crushing blow to the main force
of the American Fleet in Hawaiian waters by using the full
strength of the 1st and 2nd air Squadrons against it, and thus
to preclude the possibility of the American Fleet advancing to
take the offensive in the Western Pacific for some time."*

It was simply a case of deciding when the offensive should take place, and on the 7th of December 1941, a Sunday, at approximately 7.45 am the first wave of Japanese planes attacked Pearl Harbour. Many of the American crewmen were still sleeping and as a result 75% of the anti-aircraft guns were unmanned. The Japanese took full advantage of this and just as had been planned, the Americans were taken totally by surprise.

In less than thirty minutes the majority of the American Fleet had been destroyed by Japanese aircraft, 2,400 service men were killed, while 16 ships and over 160 planes were lost in the attack. The mission had been a complete success and as the American fleet went up in smoke the Japanese simply flew on to their next targets and in a few hours, they were delivering deadly blows to Hong-Kong, Malaysia, The Philippines, Wake and Guam.

This 'Day of Infamy' as American President Franklin D Roosevelt so eloquently described the attack on Pearl Harbour, came as a terrible shock to the politicians and people of America, as war had not actually been declared on the USA by Japan. The Japanese had planned to break off negotiations with America thirty minutes before the attack was due to take place, but the message arrived several hours after the destruction of the fleet was complete. In fact the Japanese government only drafted a declaration of war after they heard the attack on Pearl Harbour had been successful, and the American Ambassador received it in the evening of the 7th of December.

The American people were appalled and to a person, they

wanted revenge for the unprovoked attack. On the 8th of December, the day after Pearl Harbour, America officially declared war on Japan, and any thoughts of isolationism were quickly put aside. President Roosevelt at last had the backing of the American people to take up arms against Japan, and by definition the rest of the Axis Powers.

Because of the tripartite pact between Japan, Hitler and Mussolini, Germany and Italy declared war on America on the 11th of December. In these shocking few days the war became truly global, and many saw it as the beginning of the end for the Axis Powers. Churchill, as always, put the matter into focus saying this about America's decision to join the war:

> *Hitler's fate was sealed, Mussolini's fate was sealed. As for the Japanese, they would be ground to powder.*

Declarations of war now came thick and fast. Japan had also declared war on Britain, and Churchill reciprocated on the 8th of December, while the Netherlands also declared war on Japan. China officially did the same the next day, followed on the 12th of December by the USA and Britain declaring war on Romania and Bulgaria, and Hungary on the 13th. The impact that the attack on Pearl Harbour would have across the world marked the end of Hitler's total domination of Europe, and as the British looked forward to a Christmas of hope, with the promise of American reinforcements, the tide in favour of the Axis Powers was about to turn.

There has been a great deal written about Pearl Harbor and much speculation about how such an attack could have crippled the mighty American Fleet. The conspiracy theorists would have us believe that both Franklin D Roosevelt and Winston Churchill knew full well that the Japanese were going to attack Pearl Harbour on the 7th of December. After all it was certainly in Churchill's interest for the Americans to enter the war, and maybe Roosevelt felt the same way. When Churchill went to bed after the American's declaration of war he said:

"Being saturated and satiated with emotion and sensation, I went to bed and slept the sleep of the saved and thankful."

We'll probably never really know whether the rumours surrounding Pearl Harbor have any foundation, but these tactical manoeuvres will of course go down in history, as one of the war's best-kept secrets.

However, we do know that on the 17th of November 1941, the American ambassador to Japan cabled the State Department to notify them that the Japanese were planning to launch an attack on Pearl Harbour. It would seem that the cable was ignored.

That 1941 was an eventful year throughout is without question, despite the fact that the most significant event did not take place until December. Conflict in the Balkans and in Russia meant that Hitler's military forces were far more stretched than they had ever been and with Mussolini unable to play his part in Africa, German reinforcements had been required there too. Hitler was also more pro-active with racial hygiene, rounding up large numbers of Jews, and devising methods for their mass executions.

It's interesting to note that during the First World War when Adolf Hitler was fighting for his adopted German homeland, he already had highly developed anti-Semitic views. Some theorists believe this may have been triggered by his father's illegitimacy, as there have been suggestions that Hitler's paternal grandfather was actually a Jew.

However it was far more likely to have been the company Hitler kept as a struggling artist in the land of his birth, Austria, that influenced him the most. He fell in with an anti-Semitic group who believed the Jews were responsible for all the nation's ills, and as soon as he could, Hitler moved to Germany, where, by the outbreak of World War I, he'd become a fierce patriot.

When Hitler was blinded by a gas attack in 1918, he had what seems to have been some kind of nervous breakdown, and while he was recovering in hospital, he shared his extreme views with those around him. Hitler believed that his purpose in life was to save Germany, and to do this he would first need to rid Europe of all Jews. Quite how he planned to do this, he didn't say, but by the end of 1941 he had created the means to finally put his plans into action, in the gas chambers of his concentration camps. Adolf Hitler had spent twenty-three years nursing his poisonous grudge and the consequences for anyone of the Jewish faith were about to become catastrophic. In fact as 1941 drew to a close, the world, now irrevocably at war, was a very dangerous place indeed, especially for anyone who stood in the way of Adolf Hitler's master plan.

What promise the New Year of 1942 would bring with it, was yet to be seen, but for Winston Churchill and the people of Great Britain, they were no longer fighting the Nazi dictator alone. During the course of the year both Russia and America had joined the Allies, and at last there was a faint flicker of light at the end of the dark tunnel of war. Adolf Hitler and his Axis Powers had between them taken on more battles than they could possibly win, and only time would tell how long it would take for them to realise this.

WORLD WAR II HISTORY JOURNALS: 1942

In the opening days and weeks of 1942 the impact of the wider world now being at war really began to be felt. Since 1939 Adolf Hitler and his Axis powers had dominated mainland Europe and for a time it seemed that every military move Hitler made was successful. By the end of 1940, the Germans had completed their occupation of France and in the autumn months, had fought the Battle of Britain with a view to an early invasion of the United Kingdom.

As an island nation, standing alone against Hitler the British faced the terror of the Blitz, as the Luftwaffe bombed London and other major cities, night after night. Under the leadership of Winston Churchill the people defiantly refused to allow their spirits to be broken, but as another year passed, the threat of a Nazi invasion force reaching Britain's shores loomed as large as ever.

However as 1941 progressed Adolf Hitler's tactical manoeuvres resulted in a complete change of focus. On the 22nd of June, Operation Barbarossa was launched, as the Nazis began a meticulously planned invasion of Russia, despite having signed a non-aggression pact with Stalin just before the outbreak of war. Then six months later on the 7th of December the Japanese, Germany's most powerful ally, attacked the American Naval fleet at Pearl Harbour bringing the United States into the conflict.

From fighting alone at the beginning of the year, Winston Churchill and the British had been joined by the world's two strongest powers by the end of it, and quite suddenly Hitler's global supremacy was no longer a forgone conclusion.

January the 1st 1942 officially saw these allied nations, who were by now resolved to rid the world of Hitler and the Axis powers of evil, formed a solid partnership. On this day Great Britain, along with the United States, Russia, China and twenty-two other countries, signed a solemn agreement that they would continue to fight the Axis powers until a united world peace was settled. With Winston Churchill and President Roosevelt at the forefront, four fifths of the world was signed into the 'United Nations'. Alone there was little many countries could do to stop Hitler's well-oiled war machine but joined together there was at last a glimmer of hope for the future of mankind.

Hitler was at his most exposed since the war began with large numbers of his troops required for Operation Barbarossa, as they would be for some time yet to come. The Germans wanted to sit securely on their winter lines in Russia and wait until the spring to carry on with their offensive, but they were simply not prepared for the harshness of the Russian winter. Combine with this the fact that their tanks kept breaking down in the sub-zero conditions and you begin to get some idea of the difficulties they faced.

The Russian Red Army however had no problem with conditions, they were well used to winter warfare, and kept going with their counter offensives. Consequently, the Nazis were in no position to fight back, and had little choice but to retreat.

It was something Adolf Hitler had been quite unaccustomed too but back home in Germany the news was very cleverly twisted by his propagandists.

There was no mention of retreat, the newscasts simply stated that Germany was *"allowing the enemy to shed his blood through this defensive action, then, at the right time, return to the offensive"*.

However the Russian casualties were horrific and the Germans, although now struggling with freezing conditions, had made big advances. During January 1942 Hitler was busy drawing up plans to complete the occupation when the spring came, bringing the better weather. In fact the Axis Powers still had the upper hand, as the Americans were yet to make their opening moves in the war, and in North Africa, the Desert Fox, Hitler's Field Marshal, Erwin Rommel, was keeping the Allies at bay.

The spread of the conflict was wider ranging than it had ever been, with the Russians fighting on home territory, the British in North Africa and out at sea pitting their wits against the German U-Boats, while the Americans battled in the Pacific. Although there were now very diverse cultures now fighting together, part of the United Nations agreement was that no individual country, would settle for individual peace. Hitler would not be able to divide and conquer, which was crucial if the Allies were going to stem the tide of Nazi domination.

Then on the 6th of January President Roosevelt announced that American forces would be sent to Britain and also pledged massive increases in war production. When the first Americans forces set foot on British soil on the 26th of January, they came prepared with a guidebook on how to behave that made for fascinating reading.

The American Servicemen, better known as GIs, were warned not to "brag or bluster", "never criticise the King or Queen" or say "bloody" in mixed company. Because the British had been living with food rationing for such a long time there was also some wise words about how to behave socially:

"If you are invited into a British home and the host exhorts you to 'eat up, there is plenty on the table', go easy. It may be the family's rations for a whole week spread out to show their hospitality."

However, there was a much more complex issue that the GIs

had to face, that caused more friction with their British hosts than anything else. With the majority of young men away in the army, navy or RAF, the arrival of smartly uniformed Americans with movie star accents certainly attracted the ladies left on the home front. With plenty of money, cigarettes, chocolate, nylon stockings and chewing gum to help them make new friends they were very popular indeed, except of course with the British men.

Soon the Americans were labelled as "Over paid, over sexed and over here", and for the rest of the war the glamour of the GIs would continue to delight the ladies, but cause friction between the Allied fighting men.

Many of the American GIs were destined to be sent to North Africa where the fighting had been escalating without any real resolution for either the Allies or the Axis powers. Nevertheless Hitler's interests in North Africa were definitely being kept alive thanks to some particularly brilliant military strategy.

Erwin Rommel was one of the Nazis most decorated commanders having led the Panzer divisions who helped crush French opposition in 1940. The 'Desert Fox' as he became known had been fighting a very successful campaign in North Africa since February the 12th 1941 and had been a constant problem for the Allied troops. Today the fighting in North Africa is often overlooked, but back in 1942 it was of vital importance. If the Allies could get control of North Africa, then it would allow them to land troops, providing easy access to the Balkans and Mediterranean.

Likewise, Hitler knew that if the Nazis dominated this area they would pose a big threat to the all-important oil reserves in the Middle East for the Allies. Even so Hitler continued to concentrate on his battles in Russia, leaving Rommel to fight his battles in the desert.

Rommel certainly rose to the challenge, fighting a valiant campaign for Hitler in Africa, while facing any number of difficulties. The Italian troops, under his command, were disillusioned as they had suffered some humiliating defeats and they were beginning to realise that they were simply being used as Nazi cannon fodder. Rommel's divisions were also not getting enough supplies sent through, yet despite such setbacks there seemed to be nothing that could stop the "Desert Fox". Back in Britain, Prime Minister Winston Churchill knew that something had to be done about Rommel and he must have been aware that the British people would be looking for answers from his war cabinet when he gave this speech:

> It is impossible to explain to parliament and the nation
> how it is our Middle East armies had to stand for four
> and a half months without engaging the enemy, while
> all the time Russia is being battered to pieces.

This was very bad for morale, because as the British public were suffering the continuing horrors of the blitz, very little progress was being made in Africa, even though it was a vital front to hold. The British kept failing in their attacks and the situation developed into something of a stalemate, just like the Germans in Russia, with soldiers simply trying to hold their lines. But Hitler's Desert Fox had much more ambitious plans and launched yet another attack before January was over. With support from the German air force and navy, and the Italians fighting more positively, Rommel achieved his objectives, and the Allies were pushed back even further, towards the border between Libya and Egypt. Again the British simply didn't have the support to retaliate and were forced by Rommel into a defensive position.

But it wasn't only in Africa that the British were coming under attack. Towards the end of January, Japanese troops were preparing to take Singapore, a country that for the last twenty years had been at the centre of the British military presence in the Far East. The Japanese had already occupied Malaysia and the invasion of Singapore now looked inevitable, and back in Britain concern was growing daily over what was happening, because if Singapore were lost any hope of maintaining a power base in the Far East would go with it.

Winston Churchill was a firm believer in the British Empire and felt any loss of territories keenly. In fact this did cause about the only tensions between America's President Roosevelt and Churchill. Roosevelt was as committed to defeating the Axis powers as Churchill was, but he would not allow his troops to be used to protect far flung corners of the British Empire, unless it happened to be part of the overall war campaign.

Consequently, when the Japanese finally did invade Singapore on the 9th of February, the British and Australian troops were left alone to fight the battle. 30,000 Japanese soldiers stormed the small island, and it quickly became evident that they had the edge over Singapore's defenders. After a few days of intense fighting the British and Australian divisions finally surrendered Singapore to the Japanese.

Many people had believed that Singapore was untouchable and a great beacon of strength in the British Empire, yet Parliament had always been unwilling to build stronger defences, and now paid the ultimate price.

Winston Churchill was well aware of the impact the fall of Singapore would have on the British public and in his first broadcast for six months he said that the heavy defeat invoked feelings of Dunkirk for him, and with heartfelt words he spoke directly to every person in Britain:

This is one of those moments when the British race can

show its quality and its genius, when it can draw from the heart of misfortune the vital impulse of victory. We must remember that we are no longer alone. Three-quarters of the human race are now moving with us. The whole future of mankind may depend on our action and on our conduct.

However, 130,000 captured Allied soldiers were about to face the most inhumane treatment at the hands of the Japanese, as prisoners of war. The Japanese were equally as brutal as the Germans were towards the Russians, and they had little respect for the captured soldiers.

For the Japanese, to surrender in battle was the ultimate dishonour. Japanese soldiers were taught that it was better to commit suicide than to be captured and humiliated by the enemy, a tradition that dated back to ancient history and the Samurai warriors. Consequently the Allied Prisoners of War suffered appalling hardship, crammed into tiny barracks, where there was little food or water and hardly any sanitation.

To make matters worse for the Allies the Japanese were able to seize the huge British arsenal that was left in Singapore. This included over 55,000 riffles with 18 million rounds of ammunition and 2,300 machine guns with half a million rounds. One of the major contributing factors to this humiliating defeat by the Japanese was the British belief that the north side of Singapore was secure. They therefore concentrated on defending the South East, so when the Japanese seized the Island's 52 British fortress guns, sadly they were all facing in the wrong direction!

The year had begun with such high hopes for the Allies, with the Americans and Russians now determined to beat the Germans, people were expecting to see instant results. Yet Hitler and the Axis powers forged ever onwards. The Germans may have been locked in a bloody battle with the Russians, but they were far from ordering a full-scale retreat. Hitler was throwing all he could at this offensive and was still positive that he could win. The Japanese were equally buoyed up with confidence and even surer of their dominance in the new Eastern Empire. The world was quickly realising that the Japanese were as ruthless as the Nazis, and the combination of the two nations in the Axis powers was very dangerous indeed.

And if the news from the Far East wasn't bad enough, the war in North Africa was going from bad to worse. For the Allies, both the Russians and the Americans saw Africa as a minor issue and a bit of a side show compared to offensives elsewhere. However for the British fighting in North Africa, this was the war, with most of the nation's troops stationed there, with the sole purpose of defeating Rommel's Africa Korps.

Erwin Rommel was without doubt an outstanding commander and his courage, speed, improvisation, quick thinking, and occasional recklessness characterized his tactics. By comparison, the British with their static positions and obvious counter offensives had little chance against such imaginative warfare and Rommel and his troops continued to dominate.

Rommel was nevertheless a gambler and most of the time it paid off, often helped by the predictable response of the British forces. To improve their position the Allies were in desperate need of a new strategy, but for the time being all they could do was hold their ground and try not to be pushed back any further.

Back in the pacific the Japanese continued to take further control of the Far East. After Singapore, the Japanese set their sights on the island of Java in the Dutch East Indies, but before they could contemplate setting foot on land, they would have to take control of the waters around the island. On the 27th of February two Dutch cruisers were blown up and sunk by the Japanese in the Java Sea, quickly followed by attacks on two British destroyers, the Electra, and the Jupiter.

The occupation of Java and the neighbouring islands of Bali and Timor were of huge importance to the Japanese, because they were the last significant land masses before Australia, where Japan intended to invade next.

After gaining control in the Java Sea, the island itself surrendered just a few days later on the 7th of March. At midday, the Netherlands News agency stationed out in Java made its last Bulletin to the troops, by simply closing with the words, "now we shut down, long live our Queen. Goodbye till better times" and with that another country fell from Allied control and into the hands of the Axis.

For the people of Britain there was little to be cheerful about in the news. Reports of atrocities committed by the enemy were coming in almost daily, and those with loved ones captured in the Far East could only hope for a speedy conclusion to the war.

Life on the home front in Britain had changed a great deal by 1942 as people needed to use all their ingenuity to keep the nation running. As was pointed out to the American GIs, food was a major issue because of rationing and waste of any description was abhorred. When rationing first started in 1939, it was petrol that was targeted, but in 1940 bacon, butter and sugar were the earliest foodstuffs to be rationed.

In that same year meat was next, followed by tea and margarine. As supplies became even more limited in 1941 jam, cheese, and eggs were rationed, while halfway through the year clothing coupons were introduced and coal was restricted in exactly the same way.

As 1942 progressed, rice, dried fruit, soap, tinned tomatoes, peas, sweets, chocolates, and biscuits would all be rationed along with gas and electricity. Life was definitely getting tougher and the call up age was lowered to 18, so that more troops could be mobilized.

As the nation got used to living without their men folk the people left behind, all adapted to play their parts. The women, who worked tirelessly to feed their families and keep them clothed, also took jobs in factories and on the land to keep production going. The conflict gave them a real opportunity to take an active role in the war effort and make a positive contribution, and while some worked making military armaments others actually joined military organisations based in Britain.

The Women's Auxiliary Air Force, or WAAF for short, were a shining example of just how much the women of Britain could do when given the opportunity. The WAAF helped lift the barrage balloons that protected the cities from low flying bombers as well as manning the anti-aircraft guns. The war was giving women an independence and purpose that the male dominated society of the early 20th Century had never before permitted.

More and more women were seen driving buses, ambulances and taking on the roles traditionally filled by men. Even the future Queen Elizabeth II, as a young woman registered for war service, setting a fine example to the nation just as her parents, King George VI and Queen Elizabeth had throughout the Blitz.

Although both the RAF and the Luftwaffe were at first hesitant to begin bombing civilian areas in 1939, it had by now become a key tactic for all combatants, and many attacks were simply made in revenge for previous raids by the opposition.

On April the 23rd the Luftwaffe began their Baedeker raids on British cities, named after the famous German travel guides. The terror attacks were given this curious name by the deputy head of the German foreign press department who said, *"Now the Luftwaffe will go out for every building marked with three stars in the Baedeker"*. The Nazis wanted revenge for the destruction of their historic city, Lubeck and in retaliation the cathedral cities of Bath, Exeter and York were targeted.

These rural cities had very little importance in terms of the war effort, but it was now clear to what lengths Hitler was prepared to go to crush the spirit of the British people. The Luftwaffe were scoring more and more direct hits on their targets and the RAF believed that the Germans must have developed a new kind of electronic target beam to help them succeed with such regularity. But the Allies were also stepping up their bombing initiatives and were focusing on many more important German cities, so that every time the Luftwaffe struck Britain, the RAF were ready to retaliate tenfold.

Hitler could order these attacks on historic cities almost with a click of his fingers and the frightening reality of how much power this man had, came to light on the 26th of April. In a speech full of foreboding and warnings of what would happen if Germany lost the war, Hitler took absolute control of the nation. To mark this day a proclamation was read out to the Reichstag, stating what as Fuhrer, Hitler now had the authority to do:

> *Without being bound by existing legal regulations, in his capacity as Leader of the Nation, Supreme commander of the armed forces, head of the government, and supreme executive chief, supreme judge and leader of the party, must be in a position to force with all means at his disposal every German, whether common soldier or high official, to fulfil his duties.*

This gave Hitler the authority to abolish any laws that might have stood in his way, granting him absolute power over the life, and more importantly perhaps, death of every German, and as Hitler screamed that he would *"ruthlessly eliminate everybody who does not stand up to his task"* it was applauded with respect, although it has been recorded that the crowd's reaction lacked the now familiar hysterical and frenzied response. Maybe the people of Germany were beginning to fear that the man leading them, may have gone too far in his quest for power and world domination.

Whatever the German people might have feared on a personal level, the truth was that nobody could from this moment on, legally take issue with the Führer's plans. Could Hitler have recognised that things were going to get a lot worse before they got better? If so, he needed the assurance that his people would not be able to turn against him, and a few days after he made this announcement, Hitler began his summer offensive in the Crimea, determined to concentrate his Soviet campaign in the south of Russia.

This was however also because he needed the all-important oil fields in southern Russia, and he hoped that Rommel's Africa-Korps, who were storming across North Africa, would soon be able to make further advances into Iraq and Iran. This way the various branches of the German military machine would be able to join up in the Middle East before finishing the Russian campaign together.

By the end of May, with the better weather, the fighting that had started so well for the Red Army had taken a disastrous turn for the worse, as the Russians lost almost half a million soldiers as the Germans stepped up their attack. In North Africa, Rommel was also enjoying further victories over the Allies, and after a month of intense fighting, Hitler's "Desert Rat" had captured Tobruk, taking with it 35,000 prisoners, 70 tanks and vast quantities of vital supplies. To add insult to the Allies injury, six months into 1942, the German U-Boats were riding high having inflicted significant levels of damage on the Allies. Over 6 million tons of shipping and supplies were destroyed in 1942, which was double that of the previous two years.

As a result the Allies were desperately low on supplies and oil, and if the U-boats continued to score these hits the British were in danger of being forced out of the war. The Allies may have cracked the Enigma code in the previous year, allowing them to predict the whereabouts of the deadly German U Boats, but they were now going to have to win the battle for control of the Atlantic to stay in contention.

Both Winston Churchill and Franklin D Roosevelt were experienced politicians and knew that something had to be done quickly and effectively to improve Allied progress.

Since the Americans and Russians had joined the Allied cause, very little had gone in their favour. It was decided that new assaults must be started to stop Hitler and his compatriots in their tracks. Churchill announced to the world that together the Allies were planning "the earliest maximum concentration of war power upon the enemy", declaring that if it became necessary, a second, third and even fourth front would be opened, in the hope of trapping the Axis powers in what he called 'a ring of steel', and as the weeks and months of 1942 passed by, time was of the essence.

One of the Allies most important plans was to increase the number of their bombing raids, and the concentration. On the 30th of May they launched the first thousand-bomber raid on the city of Cologne. The aim of these new bombing initiatives was to saturate important industrial sites and also to demonstrate to the enemy just how powerful the bombing fleets at the Allies disposal could be. As the sun set, 1,047 aircraft took to the skies to bomb Cologne, with as many planes as possible gathered together for the mission, from the up to the minute Lancaster bombers, right through to obsolete and vintage aircraft.

Together this impressive fleet were able to drop a staggering 1,445 tons of bombs in just 90 minutes on the target area. In that short space of time the bombers killed 480 people, injured 5,027 and made 45,132 homeless. The loss of civilian life is always tragic, and it must have been a tough decision for Winston Churchill to take but considering that the mission successfully damaged or destroyed over 13,000 buildings, including many important industrial and chemical factories, the boost to the Allied war effort was significant.

The raid was so successful that a few days later another 1,000-bomber raid was carried out over Essen, which was the centre of German arms production.

Yet despite the valiant efforts of the Allies, the advancement of the Axis Powers reached a record high. The Germans controlled much of Europe and were well placed deep in the heart of Russia. The Japanese, because Roosevelt chose to tackle Germany first, had been left to do as they wished, and they had capitalised on their position to expand their empire and capture as much territory as possible in the pacific. However, the US Navy leaders in particular were calling for Roosevelt to begin positive action against the Japanese.

One of the main reasons for this was that American naval intelligence had discovered the Japanese were planning an attack on their Naval base at Midway, in the Pacific Ocean. The last thing America wanted was a repeat of Pearl Harbor, so the decision to go on the offensive was taken.

By the end of April 1942 the Japanese had overrun the East Indies and were without doubt looking towards launching an attack on New Guinea and Australia, again something the Allies wanted to avoid at all costs. Consequently a US task force utilised carrier-borne planes to stop the Japanese in their tracks.

This exchange known as the Battle of the Coral Sea took place between the 4th and the 8th of May and both sides suffered heavy losses. The Americans lost their much-prized carrier the USS Lexington, but overall served notice on the Japanese that they would never again have the upper hand in quite the way they had at Pearl Harbor.

Although the engagement ended without a clear winner, the Japanese claimed a tactical victory because of the USS Lexington, but the Allies were in fact strategically victorious, due to the fact that the Japanese abandoned their attempt to land troops at Port Moresby, New Guinea.

Midway as its name suggests, lies halfway between North America and Asia and in 1942 was of great strategic importance to both the Americans and the Japanese.

For many, the Battle of Midway, which took place a month after the Battle of the Coral Sea, is viewed as the pivotal naval battle of World War II in the Pacific. It was indeed a crushing defeat for the Japanese that crippled their Naval strength; however the Americans certainly didn't have it all their own way, and just as luck, or fate, call it what you will, had played a part for the British in withstanding Hitler's invasion plans, good fortune was on this occasion on the side of the Americans.

On 4th June, the Japanese began their offensive at Midway and at the outset appeared to be extremely successful. Their attack planes destroyed a great many US aircraft on the ground and despite American intelligence it looked like another disaster on the scale of Pearl Harbor was imminent. The Japanese were delighted with the results, and ordered another air attack on Midway, unaware of the 150 aircraft the Americans had sent to meet them.

The first counter-offensive towards the Japanese was launched as the planes refuelled and rearmed on their carrier ships, and their destruction appeared to be a foregone conclusion. But unfortunately for the Americans not a single plane hit its target and the Japanese shot down 35 of the 41 planes, to stay in contention.

The Japanese were soon ready to retaliate but first they had to find and destroy the American carriers that had sent the attack planes.

But to do this, the Japanese fighter pilots had to fly at sea level and this left the skies at higher altitude vulnerable, opening a window of opportunity for the American dive-bombers to attack the Japanese carriers.

Then luck came into the equation. A group of lost US planes had found the Japanese aircraft carriers by pure fluke and a little guesswork, and capitalising on the situation, delivered one of the most destructive and precise attacks in American Naval history. The 37 off-course American dive-bombers attacked the enemy carriers, with decks still loaded with planes. In just five short minutes they had destroyed and sunk three aircraft carriers and a staggering 322 planes, and as the Japanese fled, the Americans managed to sink yet another carrier and a battle cruiser.

The loss of military personal was the biggest blow for the Japanese. 307 American servicemen were killed while more than 3,000 Japanese died, many of whom were skilled fighter pilots and naval aviators that would be very difficult to replace. Even so, the Japanese were as tenacious as ever, and there would be many more naval battles fought in the Pacific before the end of the war, and although President Roosevelt was still prioritising removing Hitler from power, from 1942 onwards, he kept a very close eye on what the Japanese were doing.

Elsewhere things were also beginning to look a little brighter for the Allies. In North Africa, the balance of power was slowly beginning to shift as well.

Rommel was now distinctly lacking in resources and he had to stretch his troops over a huge area of inhospitable terrain, and because of this, the Nazi supply lines were now over 1,000 miles long.

Meanwhile the British were finding it relatively easy to inflict heavy losses on the Italian supply ships that sailed from Italy to Tripoli to meet the Africa-Korps. Also they were building some very strong defences in Egypt, and it was becoming evident that they were soon going to be more than a match for Rommel, giving the Allies a very strong foothold in Africa.

After being wrong footed by Rommel for so long, this was great news for the Allies and in particular the British, but Winston Churchill was being put under extreme pressure by Parliament to do more. He had been blamed for the fall of Tobruk earlier on in the year, and at this stage in the conflict the politics of warfare were equally as important as the practicalities.

But it wasn't only Churchill's war cabinet that needed to be inspired by his leadership; the Americans and Russians also had to feel confident that Britain was a worthy ally, rather than just a country that needed to be supported. Consequently, the campaign in North Africa became vitally important for Churchill and he opted for a change in command. General Claude Auchinleck, known to his men as "The Auk", had considered Tobruk as being of limited military importance, which had given Churchill a considerable political problem, when it was taken by Rommel.

So, after a visit to North Africa the British Prime Minister replaced Auchinleck with Major General Alexander, a distinguished commander in the BEF who had been the last British soldier to leave the beaches of Dunkirk back in 1940.

But the question of who to put in command of the eighth army still had to be addressed. Needing to see some positive results very quickly, Churchill's preferred choice was William Gott, an impetuous, charismatic character whose nickname "Strafer" suggested he was the best man for the job. Sadly, he was killed in a plane crash on his way back to Cairo, so Churchill had to think again, and Lieutenant General Bernard Montgomery was recommended.

Affectionately known by his men as "Monty", he was without doubt a great leader, but to suggest he could be difficult would be something of an understatement. It has been said that he was great to serve under, difficult to serve alongside, but hell to serve over and through the latter stages of the war it was something that the Allied commanders would just have to get used to. However, that he was vain, opinionated and loved self-promotion made him the perfect man to fight against the equally narcissistic Rommel, Hitler's "Desert Fox".

The first thing Montgomery did was get to know his men, and he did this on a very personal level, meeting soldiers in the field, and he created a spirit of unity between the different divisions of the eighth army that soon transformed the troops into a fighting force to be reckoned with.

Montgomery took command of the eighth army on the 13th of August and by the end of the month he was engaged in his first exchange with Rommel at the Battle of Alam Halfa. Montgomery's strategy allowed Rommel to bring the fighting to the British and it worked, resulting in a convincing victory for the

Allies.

Monty was criticised for not attacking the Germans in retreat, but he was already meticulously planning for a much bigger showdown with Rommel. Churchill discovered that despite giving Monty direct orders for a swift attack, he was not a man to be swayed by anyone, not even a Prime Minister, and it took until October for Montgomery to be ready for action.

By this time he had the advantage of nearly four Allied soldiers for every German, the same ratio in aircraft and three tanks to one statistic, so crucial in the desert terrain. Finally on the 23rd of October, Monty was ready for the second battle of El Alamein, in which the Allies were victorious, once again forcing Rommel to retreat. Monty had predicted that the battle would take twelve days to complete, and he was right. Although Churchill had been forced to be patient, the maverick Lieutenant General had delivered.

It was one of the most important and decisive land battles won by the Allies in the whole of World War II, and it proved to be a real turning point. Back in Britain, Monty was a national hero and promoted to the rank of full General, before receiving a Knighthood from King George VI at Buckingham Palace.

Also things were beginning to look more promising for the Allies in Russia, after the Germans had been locked in battle for the whole year without making a great deal of progress. In October, Hitler's soldiers began a siege on the city of Stalingrad, but this was far from being an important strategic city, and the siege quickly became a question of pride.

Stalingrad was one of the many cities named after Stalin and because of this, the Russian leader refused to abandon it. For the very same reason, Hitler was determined to see the city crushed and humiliated, and one of the bloodiest battles of all time was fought, hand-to-hand and street-by-street. This account written by a German soldier really paints a picture of what the conditions were like:

We have fought for fifteen days for a single house with mortars, grenades, machine guns and bayonets. Already by the third day fifty-four German corpses are strewn in the cellars, on the landings and the staircases. There is a ceaseless struggle from noon to night. From storey to storey, faces black with sweat, we bombed each other with grenades in the middle of explosions, clouds of dust and smoke. Stalingrad is no longer a town, it is an enormous cloud of burning, blinding smoke; it is a vast furnace lit by the reflection of the flames.

It took until December for the siege to collapse with the Red Army finally wearing the German invaders down. It was a crushing blow for Adolf Hitler and the Axis Powers, and the year that had started with such promise was ending in disarray. Goebbels, Hitler's minister of information and propaganda, wrote these words for his weekly newspaper article, hoping to rally the German people, but the supreme confidence that once dominated every Nazi approved utterance, was now distinctly lacking:

Wherever we look we see mountains of problems. Everywhere the path ascends at a steep and dangerous angle and nowhere is there a shady spot where we may stay and rest.

There was now a great deal at stake as the global conflict escalated with battles being fought from the warm waters of the South Pacific to the icy wastes of Stalingrad. Yet Adolf Hitler, the man responsible for triggering the outbreak of hostilities way back in 1939 was beginning to falter. Hitler's state of mind was deteriorating as his military and economic decisions became increasingly erratic, however such was his power no one dared question him.

Also his left hand had begun to shake uncontrollably, which

could well have been a symptom of Parkinson's Disease, but whatever the cause of Hitler's instability, as Fuhrer he had an uphill struggle ahead of him, and the Nazi propaganda machine went into overdrive to keep any reports of any illness suppressed.

The Allies could not have known just how much Hitler's errors of judgement had furthered their cause, but as they faced another Christmas at war, there was at last a real hope that the Axis Powers could be stopped in their pursuit of world domination.

WORLD WAR II HISTORY JOURNALS: 1943

All around the world as the new year of 1943 began, the effects of a global war were really taking a firm hold. Hardship and deprivation were now simply a way of life, but for the Jews and other ethnic and social groups targeted by Adolf Hitler's racial hygiene programme, they were literally fighting for survival. However, at least by this stage, news of the terrible atrocities committed in the ghettos and concentration camps had reached the Allies, making leaders Winston Churchill and Franklin D Roosevelt more determined than ever to end Hitler's reign of terror, with the utmost expediency.

The Allied position was stronger than it had ever been, yet Hitler and his Axis powers were still in a dominant position, even though towards the end of 1942 the chinks in the Axis armour were opening wider and wider. The German army on the eastern front were still surrounded in Stalingrad and to all intents and purposes were on the brink of defeat, while in North Africa, Hitler's "Desert Fox", Rommel and his troops were still holding some ground, but were most definitely being given a hard time by the British Eighth Army and their commander, General Montgomery.

And in the Pacific, the Japanese were still counting their losses after the Battle of Midway, as they struggled to restore their Navy and get more pilots and navigators battle ready to replace those killed in the decisive victory for the Americans.

Yet despite the strengthening position of the 'United Nations', they were still failing to work closely enough to make an impact and often seemed to be fighting their own separate battles.

To make matters worse Stalin, the Russian leader, was understandably viewed with great suspicion, having only recently joined the Allies after being part of a non-aggression pact with Hitler, and he became ever more isolated. Wars make for strange alliances, and this was especially true in 1943, as Stalin had no more respect for personal freedom than Hitler did and in practice this meant that the Western Allies kept their distance.

Because of this Stalin experienced a sense of isolation, with America and Britain reluctant to provide support for Russian troops who were fighting the Germans. Although the Red Army were doing a sterling job, pushing the Germans closer to a mass retreat across Russia, Stalin persisted in urging Churchill and Roosevelt to open a second front in Europe.

Stalin knew that if the Allied troops landed in Northern France, then Hitler would have to send many of his fighting men, engaged in the campaign against the Russians, to protect Hitler's occupied territories further west. Churchill and Roosevelt acknowledged that fighting the Nazis on more than one front was the right tactic and probably the only way to ultimately beat Hitler, but it was all a question of timing. After a great deal of arguing they decided that invading German occupied France could only be successful, if there were significant troop numbers to pose a serious threat to Hitler.

The last thing Churchill needed now was another Dunkirk at such a critical stage in the war. The rescue of more than 300,000 allied fighting men from the beaches of northern France in 1940 had been, as Churchill put it, "a miracle of deliverance", but it was the result of a crushing defeat at the hands of the advancing Nazis. A repeat performance could turn the tide of the war, now poised to go either way, back in the German's favour.

Stalin had no choice but to accept Churchill and Roosevelt's decision not to open up a second front in Europe for the time being, but this did cause some resentment as he believed that they were saving the blood of *their* soldiers, while the Russians were shedding theirs for the greater good. Nevertheless, Churchill and Roosevelt had to take great care in their treatment of Stalin, because it was vital that Russia did not make another deal with Hitler. If Russia agreed to a peaceful settlement with the Germans, it would make it a great deal harder for the British and Americans to win the war.

Despite there being differences of opinion between the Allied nations, Hitler's position was far from being unassailable and early in 1943, the Red Army made significant progress when on the 31st of January the first trapped German soldiers under siege at Stalingrad, surrendered. Stalin knew that he now had the upper hand and was ready to ensure that his army would continue to pile on the pressure to force a full German retreat along the whole of the Eastern front.

The Red Army finally won the Battle for Stalingrad on the 2nd of February with the complete destruction of the German 6th Army, as, just like Napoleon before him, Hitler had failed to subjugate the Russians in their homeland.

Meanwhile, Churchill and Roosevelt met in Casablanca to discuss the Allies next move. Stalin was invited to the Casablanca Conference, but declined; however Charles De Gaulle and Henri Giraud were both there representing the French.

While confirming that opening a second European front was not yet feasible, the Allies turned their attention to other fronts where they could strike a destructive blow. To date, Montgomery's activities in North Africa were beginning to produce results and most of the Anglo-American forces were stationed close by.

As a result. the Allies believed they would soon have control of this vital landmass, so they needed to decide what to do once

Hitler and the Axis powers had been driven out of North Africa. After lengthy discussions it was finally decided that an advance to attack Sicily and Italy would be the most logical tactical route to take, and this was one of the aims that was stated by Roosevelt in the Casablanca Declaration. The other resolutions were, firstly, the Allied demand for the unconditional surrender of the Axis, secondly, an agreement to aid the Soviet Union and lastly to settle the differences between De Gaulle and Giraud, as they became joint leaders of the Free French.

Straight away, more forces were put into the North African campaign and the Anglo-American troops continued to beat Rommel into retreat along the coast of Africa. Because of the extra concentration on this continent, by the end of January Rommel, who was very ill at the time, was forced back to Tunisia. Although German losses were escalating, Hitler had no intention of simply giving up on North Africa and he despatched a further two hundred and fifty thousand men and 400 aeroplanes to aid his Desert Fox in his campaign to win back North Africa. For a time, this improved Rommel's progress and with the welcome reinforcements he was able to launch a number of attacks with varying degrees of success.

On February the 14th the Battle of the Kasserine Pass broke out between the American 1st Armoured division and Rommel's newly replenished Panzer division. The Americans, who launched the attack, aimed to push Rommel back further towards the coast in the hope that he would soon flee the continent altogether.

But the Americans were not dealing with any normal commander and despite Rommel still being extremely ill he was able to muster a very successful counterattack. Using his preferred Blitzkrieg style of assault, Rommel was able to cut off 2,000 allied soldiers and when the American 1st Armoured division attempted to fight back, the move was badly planned, driving them directly into the German artillery, resulting in their annihilation.

This was hard hitting proof that the Germans were prepared to fight until the bitter end and were still able to inflict some very serious casualties on the Allied forces, even when the odds were against them.

The American forces had to quickly pick themselves up and learn from their mistakes. They were determined not to allow this set back to stop their mission and on the 24th of February, the United States army, led by General George Patton, eventually pushed Rommel back to where he had started his last counter-offensive. The US army learnt some vital lessons about Rommel at the Kasserine Pass, but they could not afford to have the Desert Fox outsmart them again. Then, once again, fate played a part in the Allies fortunes as Rommel's illness became worse and with reduced numbers of troops, his next four counterattacks on the Tunisian-Libyan border were unsuccessful.

Enough was finally enough for the Desert Fox, and far from being a well man, Rommel left North Africa on the 10th of March and handed over power to General Arnim, never to return again.

Meanwhile out at sea, Hitler and the Axis powers were enjoying much more success with their U-Boat offensive. Hitler knew that as long as his U-Boats remained a significant threat in the Atlantic, then an Allied invasion of Western Europe would be extremely difficult and more importantly Britain could still be annexed out of the War.

In three days of intense fighting from March the 16th onwards, the German U-Boats destroyed 32 allied merchant ships and by the end of the month they had sunk 108 ships in total. Despite the Allies best efforts it looked as if Hitler was on course to win the battle of the Atlantic. Even Churchill with his never say die attitude commented that, *"The only thing that really frightened me during the war was the U-Boat peril"*, but not of course at the time, waiting until after the conflict was over to voice his fears.

The British Royal Navy concentrated all their efforts on this problem, and they were determined not to lose this essential battle, because the consequences would be grave. Throughout April and May the extra attention that the British had focused on the Atlantic, dating right back to 1941 was slowly beginning to pay dividends. From April the all-important convoys from America were protected in a number of different ways, some technological and others tactical.

Long-range aircraft equipped with short-range radar and powerful searchlights could now easily pick up surfaced U-Boats and there were also much larger concentrations of specialist fleets that could go to the rescue of any Allied convoys under attack, while new types of bombs, carriers and message interception equipment were all used.

"Ultra" was the code name used for intelligence gathered by the British from the decryption of German communications throughout the war, basically because this was Ultra Secret rather than run of the mill Top Secret. This was still just as vital as it had been when the Bletchley Park Code breakers cracked "Enigma" in May of 1941, because much of the German cipher traffic had been encrypted on the Enigma machine. With "Ultra", the Navy were able to plot almost every U-Boat movement and attack accordingly, sending out fleets to intercept them straight away.

Also as a result of this superior intelligence, when the Royal Navy discovered that the Germans had deciphered the codes the British were using, they simply changed them to ensure that the Germans couldn't keep up with them. The Allies really were making the most of every new technological development, in stark contrast to the Germans, who had hardly made any advances with their U-Boats since they were first deployed at the start of the war.

Couple this with the fact that the Germans were now fast running out of experienced crews to man the submarines and even the Battle of the Atlantic, which had gone Hitler's way for so long, steadily turned in favour of the Allies throughout 1943.

In fact, everywhere Hitler and the Axis powers looked, what gains they had made since the outbreak of war in 1939 were slowly but surely being eroded. Many of the countries they had occupied were beginning to resist German rule. Far from making life better for the people they controlled, the German's often abused the countries they occupied, so much so that determined resistance groups formed, who would help the Allied forces in any way that they could.

Guerrilla groups were springing up all over the globe and they were all focused on defeating Hitler and the Axis powers. Some were extremely strong, like the Yugoslavian Partisans, who along with other groups in the Balkans, were keeping 60,000 Italian troops occupied, preventing them from assisting in Hitler's essential North African offensive.

Although others could not use force, as they did not have the large numbers that the Yugoslavians had, they still showed their defiance in other ways. Many groups would bravely risk their lives by informing the Allies of troop movements or by looking after any Allied forces they could. One of the main roles that these resistance groups took on was to look after those who were persecuted by the Nazis. Many small villages hid people from the Jewish community who were being systematically rounded up and killed by the regime.

The horror of the German atrocities escalated throughout 1943, especially for people of the Jewish faith. Once the Germans occupied a country and neutralised the armed forces, they would then turn their attention to the Jews, searching them out to send them to the concentration camps.

All this was part of what Hitler called the 'Final Solution' for the Jewish problem in Europe. Even before war broke out ,Hitler was determined to rid Europe of the Jews and in January 1939 during a speech in the Reichstag he stated his intentions:

> *Today I will once more be a prophet; if the international Jewish financiers in and outside Europe should succeed in plunging the nations once more into a world war, then the result will not be the Bolshevizing of the earth, and thus the victory of Jewry, but the annihilation of the Jewish race in Europe.*

The gassing and mass murder of the Jews was by now a daily reality and many death-camps were in full operation. There were killing centres all over Germany and it was thought that by the end of 1943, more than two million Jews had already been brutally murdered.

Sadly, although they now were all too aware of what Hitler was doing, there was little the Allies could do to intervene until the Axis powers were defeated. Hitler had to be beaten as quickly as possible if these terrible crimes against humanity were to be stopped. In an effort to speed up the proceedings, more American troops were being sent to North Africa to finish the task there, and it looked as though complete victory in North Africa was now extremely close for the Allies.

Even Rommel, who was now back in Berlin, was pleading with Hitler to let the troops retreat as he considered staying and fighting to be 'plain suicide'. Hitler, who had always respected

Rommel's tactical mind, believed that his recent illness had made him lose his nerve, and so dismissed Rommel's plea for the lives of his men.

Nevertheless, the strain on Hitler was beginning to show, as he now looked considerably older than his 53 years, having developed a nervous tic due to the onslaught he was facing in North Africa and Russia.

Having made such inroads, the Allies had no intention of slowing down their operations in North Africa, and thanks to Ultra they were able to second-guess almost every single air and naval movement of the Axis in North Africa. Consequently the Allies were able to destroy vital supplies to Hitler's troops who were by now almost completely cut off, and the situation got so desperate they had to resort to distilling fuel from wine and spirits, to keep their remaining 100 tanks operational.

The Axis were surrounded and couldn't even escape by sea. When Monty attacked again in early May, the Allies were able to quickly capture Tunis and a few days later on May the 13th, the Africa Korps finally surrendered. At 2.15pm a telegram was sent to Winston Churchill:

> *"Sir, it is my duty to report that the Tunisian campaign is over. All Enemy resistance has ceased. We are the masters of the North African shores".*

It was good news indeed for the British Prime Minister. Over 250,000 German and Italian troops were taken prisoner in the attack, the largest number of soldiers that had been captured by the Allies since the outbreak of war. American General, Dwight D Eisenhower, who had been instrumental in planning the Allied victory, recorded a broadcast for his countrymen back home, as both Britain and the USA enjoyed a much-needed morale boost.

This was a humiliating defeat for Hitler and the long battle in North Africa had cost the Axis over 1 million soldiers, 8,000 aeroplanes and 2 million tons of shipping. But the Allies, despite their obvious jubilation, had to maintain their momentum keeping both Hitler's and Mussolini's men on the run, before they had the chance to regroup and retaliate.

Since the shakeup in North Africa with Monty commanding the troops and the arrival of American reinforcements, victory had come relatively quickly. Speed was now of the essence and Churchill met with his North African commanders to plan the invasion of Sicily, which had been laid out in the Casablanca Declaration. Code-named Operation Husky, it was Churchill's favoured course of action, otherwise the troops would have had to return to Britain to wait for the second European front to open.

Churchill was keen for the Allies to capitalise on their advantage, and he definitely saw Italy as a backdoor into Germany, although not everyone agreed with him, but it was recognised that by occupying Italy, the balance of power could only swing even further in favour of the Allies.

Operation Husky needed to be carried out at speed because there were very few German troops in Sicily after the victory in Africa, and it was vital that the Allies struck hard and fast. However, the weeks were passing, and the invasion was yet to begin, with the clock ticking.

While all the preparations were going on for Operation Husky, another operation, code-named Chastise, was about to boost Allied morale.

Although Chastise may not sound immediately familiar, when you realise that the Royal Air Force Squadron, number 617, that carried out the mission are also known as the Dam Busters, you'll certainly have heard of them, and one of the best-known events of 1943.

On 16th May, 133 aircrew flying specially adapted Lancaster bombers, took off, for the German Ruhr area. Their targets were three Dams on the Eder River and they were carrying a revolutionary type of bouncing bomb, designed by Barnes Wallis. The mission was successful, and the resulting flooding caused havoc, and certainly hampered the German war effort.

The Dam Buster raids were however costly, with 53 of the aircrew killed and 3 captured as prisoners of war. The dashing Wing Commander in charge of the operation, Guy Gibson was awarded the Victoria Cross and became something of a celebrity, only to be killed on a mission in 1944.

For Churchill, the public relations implications could not have been better timed, helping to convince the Americans and the Russians that Britain was capable of being an effective Ally. Also for those on the home front still being bombed every night by the Luftwaffe, it felt like sweet revenge, while the hardship caused in Germany as a result dented public morale considerably. It was now becoming evident that Adolf Hitler was not as invincible as he had made everyone believe, and matters continued to deteriorate for the Fuhrer.

There was further good news for the Allies from the Atlantic on the 22nd of May, when Grand Admiral Donitz withdrew all his U-Boats from the North Atlantic. Thirty-three U-Boats had been destroyed in May alone, and to make matters worse the Germans were sinking fewer allied ships.

Donitz was forced to accept the fact that the lengthy campaign to destroy the Allied supply lines from America had failed. The submarines that were withdrawn from the North Atlantic were sent South in the hope of greater success from there, but The British Navy with Ultra, new intelligence systems and various tactical and technological innovations were always just one step ahead.

July 1943 proved to be a critical month for Hitler, as he returned to the fray, turning his attention back to the Russians. On 5th July the Battle of Kursk began, the Germans with just under half a million men, ten thousand artillery pieces and three thousand tanks attacked Kursk in a desperate effort to restore German pride. This was Operation Citadel and after four days of fighting in what proved to be the world's largest tank battle, the Red Army stopped the Germans dead in their tracks, having taken only twelve miles of land.

While the Germans were slowing down in Russia, the Americans were only just getting started in the Pacific. It was essential to step up operations, to at the very least, keep the Japanese under control until the war in Europe had been won. The Americans had been working hard to push the Japanese back towards their homeland, starting with the Battle for the East Solomons in August.

Through the course of many sea battles the Americans hoped to push beyond the Solomon Islands towards New Guinea, and then reach the Philippines before moving towards mainland Japan. The American Admirals called the tactic 'leapfrogging', as the US forces would hop from island to island as they pushed ever closer to Japan. The many Islands that are scattered across the Pacific actually helped the Americans in their campaign. The only way to get supplies and men onto an occupied Island at speed and in any numbers was by carrier.

However these were easy targets for the American dive-bombers and after several losses the Japanese no longer dared to send in ships when the Americans were on the offensive. This meant that once the Americans were attacking an island all they needed to do was neutralise the stronghold from the air or sea, before moving onto the next one. They could safely do this because the Japanese would not risk their shipping to counter-attack.

During 1943 the Pacific Ocean was a busy place, and not just in the south; further north the activities of the US Navy were just as strategic. There were American divisions positioned on a number of the Aleutian Islands and from here the Americans could now move down from the north, to close in on the Japanese from two sides.

The Americans had a luxury that few other countries could afford at the time, which was a seemingly endless supply of men and armaments. By 1943 the Americans were producing over 85,000 aircraft, which was almost as many as Britain, Russia, Germany, and Japan put together, and they were also leading the way in shipping and tank production. Because of these huge numbers and no shortage of men enlisting in the armed forces, the US were able to position men on many vital fronts, all around the world.

As the American forces were hard at work dominating the North and South Pacific, they were also ready to take part in the invasion of Sicily on the 10th of July. The Allies had been preparing for many weeks by carrying out air raids on the island and neutralising the Luftwaffe. When the enemy positions in Sicily were sufficiently damaged, it was time for one of the greatest seaborne invasions of the war. As 3,000 ships headed towards the Mediterranean Island, many of the soldiers, who would have been rescued from Dunkirk some three years earlier, were ready to face the Germans once again on occupied soil. By dawn, Operation Husky was going to plan, and 150,000 allied troops were safely ashore, with 320,000 ready to join them over the next two days.

To begin with it appeared that the invasion forces were going to meet with little in the way of resistance. The storms that had been savaging the Mediterranean for days before the invasion, made the Italians believe that any Allied landings would be impossible in such conditions. Consequently many of them were simply sleeping, only to wake and surrender straight away, as they were caught off guard. The Italians didn't even believe an Invasion was likely, as the Allies had used very effective methods of deception to ensure there would be minimal forces stationed on Sicily to ward off any attack.

The Allies used a corpse dressed as a British soldier and placed it in the sea just off Spain with false documents to make the Germans and Italians believe that the Allies were planning an invasion of Sardinia and Greece. Hitler was informed of the find, and the contents of the documents, and because of this a panzer division was dispatched to the Balkans, and German warships sailed from Sicily to Sardinia.

As a result of this Hitler only had two divisions left stationed out on Sicily, but they were not to be underestimated, being veterans from the war in North Africa, and some of his finest soldiers. They might have only been small in numbers, but they could still prove to be a formidable threat.

The plan was that Allied troops would land in the Southeast and west of the Island, then the Divisions could head as quickly as possible for Messina, preventing many of the Axis forces from escaping to Italy via the Messina straits. The advancements of the British 8th Army in the south and the US 7th Army in the west was not as speedy as had been hoped for, and they didn't reach Messina until the 17th of August. This was due to the brilliant resistance of the German soldiers and the logistic problems that the natural rocky terrain of the Island caused.

Because of the difficulties more than 110,000 Axis soldiers were able to escape safely to Italy. Operation Husky, although successful, was a tough campaign, and it showed the Allies that the Germans and Italians were not totally beaten, and that they needed to be prepared for what might be a long battle to make their way up through Italy. The Allies knew they would have to keep piling on the pressure if they stood any chance of crushing Hitler's New World Order.

To make matters worse, American General George S. Patton, who had successfully commanded the US 7th Army in the mission, was replaced by a less effective General. Eisenhower, who was his commander, had a very difficult incident to deal with when Patton visited an army hospital to commend the men for their bravery.

When he encountered two men with shell shock, what today we would describe as Post Traumatic Stress, he slapped the two US soldiers and shouted abuse at them. The outburst almost ruined the controversial General, but when Eisenhower suggested he apologise to the men personally in front of all those who had witnessed the bizarre event, Patton did as he was told. Ironically, Patton could well have been suffering from Post-Traumatic Stress himself, and Eisenhower's timely intervention meant that he could call on Patton at a later date, when a full-scale Allied invasion of Europe was ordered.

Meanwhile back in Russia, the Red Army were continuing to push back the Germans and seemed to be making daily gains, and then on the 23rd of August, a massive 224-gun salute was fired in Moscow to signal the recapture of the important Ukrainian city of Kharkov. On the same day, British Prime Minister Winston Churchill, American President Roosevelt, and the Canadian Prime Minister Mackenzie King officially announced that a second front would be opened in France, against the Germans, as momentum gathered for the Allies.

But it wasn't only in Europe that advances were being made. In the Pacific, the Americans were continuing to fight with great success. On the 4th of September Allied troops seized a key port in New Guinea. Australian and American troops, just as had happened in Sicily, used counterintelligence tactics rather than brute force to achieve their objective. The Australians covered up their plan to attack the port of Lae by threatening the nearby town of Salamaua.

The Japanese, logically, took defences away from Lae to protect the threatened town, so when the Allies landed, they met little resistance, and continued to push ever closer towards Japan.

Back in Europe, on the 3rd of September the first few allied troops landed at the toe of Italy and the invasion of the mainland seemed as if it would be swift and easy. Some Italian soldiers even helped to unload the allied ships. The Italians no longer wanted to fight Hitler's battle, and on the same day they secretly signed an Armistice with the Allies in Sicily.

The wind of change was sweeping across Italy. Benito Mussolini was stripped of his power in July, and now many of his countrymen viewed him as the most hated man in Italy. Mussolini had promised the Italians victory and a new empire, instead all he had delivered were humiliating defeats in East Africa, Albania, Greece, Egypt, Libya, and Tunisia.

On the 8th of September, the Armistice was made official, and Germany's former partner surrendered its forces unconditionally to the Allies. A day later Allied troops landed in large numbers along the west coast of Italy in what was recorded to be a 'holiday spirit'. Many of the British and American forces, who had just heard the good news, were dangerously relaxed as they came ashore.

However as the jubilant men walked on the beaches, they quickly realised that although the Italians were now out of the war, the Germans were not. They had anticipated the Italian surrender and were quickly placing reinforcements in Salerno, where four Panzer divisions were all ready and waiting.

The Germans also swiftly occupied Rome and despite five Italian divisions being placed there to protect the city from their old brothers in arms, they were soon overpowered by the Nazi invaders. The Germans were disgusted by what they considered to be the Italians cowardly way out of the war, and brutally dealt with any Italian soldiers who tried to put up a fight as they were being disarmed.

Consequently the invasion of Italy did not go precisely to plan for the Allies, despite the Italian forces having already surrendered, and further developments were making the Ally's job much harder. On the 12th of September in a brilliant airborne raid, the German SS rescued Mussolini from where he had been detained in a mountain prison. He was then reinstated by the Nazis as dictator, and in Northern Italy a violent war broke out between the antifascist Italian Partisans and Mussolini's fascist militia, with the help of German troops.

Italy was now practically a German occupied country, and to make matters worse in the north, there was now civil war. The bloodshed, which the Italian government and Allied forces had hoped to avoid when they embarked upon the invasion, was now inevitable and moving up through Italy was going to be much harder than had been expected. The Allies were hoping to reach Rome by the end of the year; however they would not actually see the Gates of the city until the June of 1944.

But this was only a part of a much bigger picture and the Allies continued their bombing raids on enemy cities. They were continuously stepping up their bombing initiatives and were now attacking the Mediterranean as well as Europe.

New and ever more destructive bombs were being produced and 1943 was the year when major efforts were made by the Americans, developing their nuclear program, to produce an atomic bomb.

Many important German cities now lay in ruins and millions of German families had to be evacuated, causing terrible hardship for the civilian population caught up in the conflict. Sadly, this, as always, was the price of warfare. Yet if there was to be an Allied victory, removing the threat of Adolf Hitler to world peace, for good, it was a cost that had to be born. As one RAF pilot so eloquently put it, *"No regrets, remember what the Nazis did to London"*, and it was a sentiment that the Allies had to take to heart if they were going to march on to victory.

Back in Italy, a bloody battle for Salerno was being fought, with the Germans taking the upper hand on many occasions. However, with the equipment and personnel the Allies now had at their disposal, they were able to crash through the defences and head towards Naples. When the Allies did reach Naples, they found that the Civil War, which was being fought in the north of Italy, had now spread south and Naples already looked like a war zone.

Hundreds of Partisans lay dead in the streets, while the City had been battered to ruins by Allied bombing raids and German soldiers destroying the city so that there would be little of military use when the Allied tanks came rolling in.

The civilians of Naples were in dire need, the fighting had destroyed the sewage systems and the one million people who lived there were now threatened by outbreaks of deadly epidemics, and food was in very short supply. For the Allies it was another stark reminder that in war civilians are always the hardest hit.

The Germans had already moved to the north of the city to ensure they held a good defensive line, so there was very little fighting in the streets of Naples between the Germans and Allies. The autumn weather was now beginning to set in, and this coupled with the hilly terrain was slowing the Allied force's progress.

But there were no such setbacks for the Americans in the Pacific, as they continued beat back the Japanese. Despite their Europe first strategy the Americans had become a powerful force in the Pacific and were determined to keep the Japanese threat at bay.

Their power and sheer weight of numbers meant that they could advance with two thrusts in the South Pacific. One task-force could work up from New Guinea, while the other moved across the centre. The Americans were gaining considerable ground and their island-hopping tactic was proving to be extremely successful. Churchill was so positive about an Allied victory, that for the first time he set up a meeting to discuss how the Pacific must now be officially tackled.

On the 25th of November in Tehran, Churchill and Roosevelt met with the Chinese leader Chiang Kai-Shek to discuss what the next moves would be in the Pacific. The Allied leaders knew that the time to strike had never been more auspicious, and that 1944 would be a vital year in their campaign.

A few days later, Stalin made his first journey outside of Russia since 1917, to join Churchill and Roosevelt in Tehran to discuss in greater detail the second front in Europe. After some intense talks, an announcement was made stating that the three leaders:

Have concerted plans for the destruction of the German forces. We have reached complete agreements as to the scope and timing of the operations, which will be undertaken from the east, west and south.

They talked about the second European front, that would definitely happen in 1944, and also made it clear that the Allies would continue to work their way up through Italy to meet the Germans in the south. Stalin also agreed that once German forces were beaten in Russia, he would turn his attentions to the battle against the Japanese.

The tide had truly turned for the Allies, and Hitler and his Axis powers' dreams of world domination now looked unlikely to become a reality. As 1943 drew to a close, the Russians were celebrating a year of advances for the Red Army as the Germans were pushed ever further back towards Poland. Next Stalin was planning to clear the Ukraine early in 1944, before marching into Poland, Romania and finally Germany itself.

But unfortunately in Italy the Allied advances were not going quite so well, however things were progressing, if a little slowly, and this was a time of great hope. The Allies were not yet in Rome and the Germans were putting up a brave fight, and by the end of the year the Allies had only managed to advance 70 miles north of their main landing points in Salerno.

Nevertheless, although they may not have been moving at Blitzkrieg speed, they were still making progress and the Germans were continuing to slowly retreat. Also, at the Tehran Conference the finer details of Operation Overlord had been laid down, and the campaign was really beginning to gather momentum. For this to become a decisive action, that would herald the end of the war, a truly, massive invasion force would have to be ready before the middle of 1944 in order to take Hitler and the German army by storm.

On Christmas Eve it was announced that the man chosen to be the Supreme Allied Commander in Europe was American General Dwight D Eisenhower, who had been responsible for overseeing Operation Husky. There had been some disagreement between Roosevelt and Churchill over this, as the British Prime Minister preferred General Montgomery, but in the end, it was Stalin who had the casting vote.

That Eisenhower was capable was beyond question, with his affable style and quiet confidence, and as he had already proved he could handle commanding such diverse characters as the difficult "Monty" and "Old blood and guts" Patton as the American General was nicknamed, it was, with the benefit of hindsight a very good choice. The task ahead was so great that all of these men would need to work together if Hitler were to be beaten, and there was none more qualified to lead them than Eisenhower, despite the fact he had not seen active service in his entire military career.

The newly appointed Supreme Allied Commander of Europe was a superb administrator and strategist, and the responsibility for winning the peace now lay squarely on his shoulders, as 1944 promised to bring with it fresh hope for an Allied victory.

WORLD WAR II HISTORY JOURNALS: 1944

1944 was a year that began full of promise for the Allies as the war was beginning to slip from the grasp of Adolf Hitler and the Axis powers, and many believed that by the end of year, peace might well be restored throughout Europe. During 1943, the fifth year the world had been at war, the Allied nations had at last turned the tide against Hitler and it was now time to consolidate their much-improved position.

Germany, after bitter hand-to-hand fighting, and terrible casualties on both sides, had been forced to retreat from Russia, after the Battle of Stalingrad and with the Red Army poised to now push into Poland, the Nazis were quite literally on the run. Likewise, the Allies were making good progress in Italy since the fall of Rommel's Africa Korps in 1943. The North African conflict involved many tough desert engagements and at one point it looked as though Rommel's superior military leadership was going to guarantee another Axis victory on this all-important, but often overlooked continent.

However, with grit, determination, and clever strategy, with the Allies led by such legendary Generals as Montgomery, from Britain, and Eisenhower, from America, the Africa Korps finally surrendered, as the Axis fled to Sicily. The Allies then continued their push into Europe, invading first Sicily and then Italy, for a campaign that was expected to be swift, but progress was slower than had been hoped for.

As 1943 drew to a close, it had been hoped that the Allies would be in Rome by January, but as 1944 began, they were still locked in a desperate battle in central Italy and were many miles from the historic capital.

Also fighting was still intense in the Pacific, where the American Navy had been battling the Japanese, ever since the devastation of Pearl Harbor had brought the USA into World War II at the end of 1941.

Nevertheless the Allied leaders Winston Churchill, Franklin D Roosevelt and Joseph Stalin had all taken time out from their individual schedules at the end of 1943 to agree an Allied invasion of France, to take place in 1944, and consequently plans for Operation Overlord, the code name for the long-awaited invasion, were beginning to get underway.

If the Allies were looking for good omens, they didn't have to wait very long because on the 6th of January, a number of Russians managed to push across the border into German occupied Poland, as a complete retreat of Nazi troops from Russia was fast becoming a reality. Even Adolf Hitler's propaganda machine could no longer hide the fact that his armies were in disarray, as typified by this press statement explaining their position at this point:

> *The German high command will make no effort to hold Russian territory purely for reasons of prestige. Should the German army be compelled to retreat altogether from Russian soil, this would be only a secondary question compared with the importance of maintaining the front intact all along the line.*

Hitler's ever expanding German Empire was finally being clawed back, and his troops, far from returning to the fatherland as conquering heroes, were now retreating in defeat.

The Red Army had taken back 400 miles of land in just six months and if they continued at the same rate, they would not only push through Poland, but also take the fighting to the Germans on their home soil as well.

But the Allied operation in Italy was meeting much greater resistance and the troops were still sixty miles from the German defences on the Gustav Line, just south of Rome. The Allies therefore knew that they needed an element of surprise if they were to take Rome in the near future, so on the 22nd of January Operation Shingle was instigated with the Allied landings at Anzio, a western port just 32 miles from Rome.

The landings were a resounding success and when the 243 ships, complete with the 50,000 men arrived, there was little resistance as the Allies made their way up a deserted beach. In fact only 13 men were lost in the landings, the majority as a result of landmines. Yet the Allies failed to seize the initiative, and instead of breaking out quickly towards Rome, the commanders spent days strengthening their beachhead. This proved to be a costly mistake and although tactics and preparation are key in any military operation, speed was far more important on this occasion.

Without speed, Hitler's Blitzkrieg attacks with his Panzer divisions never would have taken Europe by storm back in 1939, nor would the Japanese have caused such a stir in the Pacific. The decision not to attack straight away was without doubt contributory to the length of time it would eventually take for the Allies to reach Rome, but back in Russia the Red Army had an equally prolonged fight on their hands at Leningrad.

On 27th January, the Russians finally broke the siege of Leningrad, which had lasted an astonishing 872 days.

The lives of over one million civilians were lost and the city had been decimated, yet for those who survived, at last, here was living proof that Hitler's regime could be beaten. The Red Army was equally active in the south of Russia, and all the Germans could really do was hold ground. Concentrating on building fortifications in specific towns, the Nazis attempted to stem the tide, but the truth was the Axis powers in Russia were slowly but surely being forced into retreat.

Even so Hitler's troops were still digging in and fighting back in Italy. Considering their decreasing numbers, they were efficiently dealing with the Allied landings, proving that Adolf Hitler and the Nazis could never be underestimated. The Germans were resisting every attack that the Allies launched from their Anzio beachhead, effectively containing them at every possible opportunity. The Nazis were so confident that they could continue to hold Italy that on the 3rd of February Hitler ordered a counterattack, demanding that the Anzio beachhead *"must be crushed in the blood of British soldiers"*.

The Allies now found themselves on the defensive in Italy and had to fight hard to beat off Hitler's counterattacks. Both sides were locked in an inevitable stalemate and both sides suffered high levels of casualties. The counterattacks were nevertheless more costly for Hitler, because he couldn't afford heavy losses at this crucial stage in his campaign, because unlike the Allies, who could call in more American troops when needed, the Germans were already overstretched, with nothing in reserve.

The same problems were facing Hitler's Axis partners, the Japanese in the Pacific, who were finding it impossible to protect all the islands they had previously seized. The Americans with their massive Navy could continue to 'island-hop' with great success and were constantly launching attacks on the Pacific Islands. A major target in the sights of the US Navy were the Marshall Islands in the central Pacific, and with 297 ships, over 1,000 aircraft, all supported by more than 54,000 men, the Americans took the Islands by force, with the first island secured at record speed without a single US loss.

At this stage the Americans knew that until Europe was liberated they would have to fight on against the Japanese without Allied reinforcements, so containment was vital throughout 1944, while Operation Overlord became the Ally's main focus.

The positive news from the Pacific would certainly help the Allied cause, but it was essential the British in Italy stepped up a gear. Winston Churchill, Britain's Prime Minister was furious over what little ground the Allies had taken since Operation Shingle was launched, declaring that: *"we hurled a wildcat on the shores of Anzio and all we have is a stranded whale"*.

Churchill was always conscious of how small the British forces were compared to the Americans and Russians, and he wanted to prove that what they might lack in numbers they made up for in courage and ability. The Allies in Italy had been pushed back towards the sea and there was now much more than gaining ground at stake. The RAF stepped up their bombing campaigns over vital Italian locations in the hope of breaking down German defences to allow the Allies the time they needed to break-out from their beachhead.

The bombing raids along with an injection of more Allied troops ensured that on the 2nd of March the Germans had to call off their offensive at Anzio. The Allies continued with this successful offensive method, intensively bombing the area they intended to advance into, for a number of days prior to moving their troops. Hitler's Axis powers in Italy were at last being neutralised and if the Allies could just keep up the momentum, Rome was now within their grasp.

Elsewhere, the Allies stepped up their air attacks over Germany, as bombing became more vital than ever, as an integral part of the campaign against Adolf Hitler. Ironically, there were plenty of folk on the home front who opposed these raids on ethical grounds, because so many innocent civilians were losing their lives, but after so long at war, it was becoming an inevitable price that would have to be paid.

In the spring of 1944, Berlin was a major target for the Allies and Air Chief Marshall Arthur "Bomber" Harris said that Berlin should be bombed until *the heart of Nazi Germany ceased to beat*. Whatever reservations were felt about the Allied bombing tactics, the general consensus was now that it was time to simply win the war as quickly as possible, and bombing, although an indiscriminate attack, caused the maximum amount of damage, at devastating speed.

Interestingly, after the war, there was a sense of national guilt over these air attacks, and "Bomber" Harris was the only major British commander not to be awarded a peerage, while the bomber aircrews were also denied a distinctive medal of their own.

Whatever we today consider to be the rights or wrongs of bombing civilian targets, in 1944 the time had come for the Allies to do whatever was necessary to stop Adolf Hitler and his megalomania, and as plans for Operation Overlord were being completed, the outcome of World War II could still swing in either direction.

The man charged with the weighty task of being Supreme Allied Commander of the Allied Expeditionary Force was American General Dwight D Eisenhower, who had already proved himself capable of handling the likes of the opinionated Montgomery and the flamboyant Patton.

Interestingly Eisenhower, unlike those he had commanded so successfully, had not seen active service, but was a superb administrator with the added bonus of an affable personality. His efforts to meet the men he commanded in the field were greatly appreciated and as the preparations for Operation Overlord came to fruition, every single one of them, from the lowest rank to a five-star General, would be needed if the Allies were going to win the war.

One of the most important decisions had been about which route the proposed invasion of France should take. Some favoured the shortest option, from Calais to Dover, which is what the Germans anticipated, but the actual destination selected was the Normandy coast, between Caen and Cherbourg. To throw the Germans off the scent though, for every air recognisance flight over Normandy, two flew over The Pas de Calais, and it was a ploy that evidently worked.

Once in France the troops would breakout from the beaches with two thrusts, meeting up to march on the vital coal producing area of the Ruhr in Western Germany before marching into the German heartland and finally, Berlin.

But there was one major obstacle that had to be overcome before the advance on Normandy could be achieved. Along the beautiful coastline there was a distinct shortage of harbours, making the invasion plan logistically very difficult. A number of highly skilled engineers came up with the idea of using a floating harbour, and two of these floating harbours, or mulberries as they were code named, were created, one to be located in the American sector and the other in the British.

With the plan for D-Day set, the Allies now needed to concentrate on gathering up the men and machinery required, and perhaps even more importantly keep the whole operation hidden from German intelligence. Eisenhower envisaged the eventual landing of over two million troops onto the beaches of Normandy, so soldiers were flown in from America, Canada, and other Allied nations. The men were greeted with jubilant cheers by British civilians as they headed for the south coast, where they would be stationed until the time was right for Operation Overlord to proceed.

While the Allies were hard at work making their preparations, the Germans in France were working equally determinedly to be in a position to thwart the invasion that they knew was coming.

Despite Rommel's failure to hold the North African territories for Hitler, the Desert Fox, as he was affectionately known, was still one of Hitler's most prized commanders, and he was put in charge of organising the German defences in France. However, after so many years at war, the Nazis didn't have the time or resources to protect their territory sufficiently.

They had no idea as to where the Allies would attack so had to stretch their defences thinly across the beaches of Northern France, and many of the German bunkers were built on or above beaches that not a single Allied soldier would step foot on. Even so, with all the defensive precautions Rommel was putting in place, Hitler was now very confident about the whole matter, certain that a cross-channel invasion would be stopped, so that all the divisions he had brought to France could be returned to the Russian Front.

Across the English Channel though, Winston Churchill was feeling nowhere near as optimistic. He was concerned that the invasion plan was too grand and if the Allies put everything they had into this operation, and it failed, the war would be lost. However, persuaded by the Americans and Russians to go ahead with Operation Overlord, Churchill once more rallied the people of Britain to give everything for this make-or-break mission.

As spring and summer of 1944 approached, the Allied soldiers worked constantly to increase their skills and knowledge of warfare. They were frequently reminded of the vital importance of this mission, and Eisenhower made numerous visits to the troops to ensure that all was going to plan.

By May the forces in Britain were ready for anything, they had trained long and hard for many months and were fully prepared for the invasion. Also, thousands of ships, aircraft and vehicles had congregated along the south coast, and Eisenhower seemed suitably impressed with what had been achieved, joking that it was *"only the number of barrage balloons floating constantly in British skies that kept the island from sinking under the waves."*

Everywhere people looked there was row upon row of military equipment and British civilians got used to sharing their island with this impressive arsenal. The allies had gathered 1200 fighting ships, 12,000 aircraft, 4,000 landing aircraft and 800 cargo ships. This was beyond anything the Germans could counter-attack with, as they no longer had the raw materials or manpower, for such an enterprise.

But before any invasion could begin in earnest, the Allies had to clear the path for the landing parties. The American and British air forces carried out a number of bombing raids on significant German held targets in France, including the all-important French railways, which the Germans relied on for transporting supplies. The French Resistance also played their part on the ground as they eagerly waited for the Allies to liberate them from the much-hated Nazi occupation, an indignity they had now suffered since 1940.

Keeping Operation Overlord secret was not an easy task, with so much activity going on in southern England, with so many men and so much equipment, and there was an incident, that to this day has never been explained, that suggested the Germans knew the whole plot.

In a series of crosswords in The Daily Telegraph, code words used for the forthcoming invasion started to appear. First of all the codenames for two of the landing beaches appeared together, Utah and Omaha, making British Intelligence very suspicious indeed. Then when the word Overlord itself appeared in the same crossword with Mulberry, the codename for the artificial harbours, alarm bells really did start ringing.

But no one was more surprised than the English teacher who set the clues when MI5 arrived at his house to question him! In the end the incident was put down to co-incidence, but so close to D-Day it was very worrying indeed.

Fortunately for the Allies, events were looking brighter elsewhere in Europe as the British and American forces were finally making headway in Italy. The Allies had an incredibly tough time in Italy, but their efforts finally paid off when they captured Rome on the 4th of June. The two million Roman civilians were ecstatic with the arrival of the Allied troops, as one of the most important cities held by Hitler and his Axis powers had been liberated.

The pope even joined in the celebrations by announcing "*Yesterday Rome was trembling for her sons and daughters. Today she is able to look with renewed hope and faith to her salvation*". As the Germans retreated further to the north of Italy to take up their defensive lines, the freedom of Rome, just a day before Operation Overlord was due to proceed, must have appeared to be a very good omen indeed.

All that was now needed was the order to go, as the Allied troops were moved into position ready to respond to the call that would ultimately determine the outcome of World War II.

But despite the meticulous preparation, planned to coincide with the best possible tides, the elements took a hand in history. As the 5th of June dawned it was evident that what should have been pleasant early summer weather, was anything but. The storms hitting the south coast of England and the north coast of France were horrendous, and definitely unseasonable, in fact, the last thing that anyone could have predicted. Consequently, with all the troops already aboard their ships, Operation Overlord had to be postponed, but the window of opportunity for the Allies was very small indeed.

The invasion force had to set out when there was a low tide in the early hours of the morning. The only days in June that allowed for this were the 5th and 6th and then the 19th and 20th and the prospect of keeping the Operation secret for another two weeks was not an option anyone wanted to contemplate.

When the forecast was little better for the next day, and Eisenhower was told of a small gap in the bad weather that gave Overlord a slim chance, he gave the order to go, as D-Day, the 6th of June 1944 went down in history.

Even so, the atrocious weather wasn't all bad news for the Allies, because it really did mean they had the element of surprise on their side. Rommel was so convinced the Allies would not attempt an invasion in such poor conditions, he actually went home to Germany for his wife's birthday party. The Germans had also been tipped off about the radio messages that would be broadcast by the BBC to let the French Resistance know that the invasion was coming, and even when this happened, on the 1st and the 5th of June, the Germans still refused to be believe the Allied troops were on their way.

As the ships sailed across the stormy sea the men had a little time for thought and reflection. The assault of German aircraft that the Allies were expecting were nowhere to be seen, and with the antiaircraft guns pointed to the skies, not a single shot was fired. Much of this was due to the remarkable achievements of the RAF, with their Spitfire and Lancaster bombers, making sure that not one Luftwaffe plane flew over the invasion fleet, because this would have without doubt given the Germans notice that they were about to be attacked.

Interestingly, although when you mention D-Day people think first of the Navy and the Army, the air forces of Britain and America made vital contributions to the success of Operation Overlord. The American Air Force dropped paratroopers into the area around Cherbourg, close to the beaches of Utah and Omaha, where the American troops were due to come ashore. Sadly, many paratroopers drowned as Rommel had flooded any suitable landing areas in the district, and one of the paratroopers, Private Steel, famously got caught on the Church spire at Saint Marie Eglise, where to this day a replica of him can be found, to commemorate the events of D-Day.

At the other end of the landing beaches, near Caen, the British 6th Airborne Division were given the task of taking a strategically important bridge, after landing under the cover of darkness in silent Horsa gliders. Major John Howard and his men landed on target, and won the first victory of the Normandy campaign, achieving their objective, and ever since this has been known as Pegasus Bridge, in honour of the flying horse insignia of the British 6th Airborne Division.

Back at sea as the invasion fleet got ever closer to the beaches of Normandy the Germans finally realised what was happening and they launched everything they could at the Allies. The sea was covered with a thick, dark smoke as both sides tried to inflict the greatest amount of damage possible before the ships reached land. The Germans had spent many years building up their empire and were not about to give everything up without a fight.

The Allies were however well prepared, and battleships and aircraft worked tirelessly to prepare the way for the landing craft. So once the smoke began to settle the first carriers were edged closer to the beaches, covering a fifty-mile stretch of coastline with five main landing beaches. From Utah and Omaha, where the Americans would land through to Gold, Juno, and Sword, where the British and Canadians would fight, the task ahead was colossal, and unfortunately the poor weather took its toll, as the landing craft were tossed about like corks in the choppy sea, and there was hardly a soldier who wasn't sick, before reaching the beaches.

When the doors of the landing craft swung open, the troops, who had been aboard ship for over 70 hours, spilled out, wet, cold, and seasick, unaware of what kind of reception was there to meet them. The men wadded through the water and headed to the beaches as quickly as possible, and what they encountered depended as much upon luck as judgement. Some of the beaches, most notably Utah, were relatively unprotected and the Allied losses were minimal, while other soldiers wouldn't even have a chance to get out of the water before being gunned down by the Germans.

The worst conditions were faced by the American troops who landed on Omaha beach, where they were met by an elite German Infantry division on manoeuvres in the area, and almost 3,000 American soldiers were slaughtered within a matter of hours.

The storms were also inflicting serious damage on the landing craft, and many of them capsized in the rough sea, as soldiers had to be dragged to safety. Also the intelligence the Allies had received wasn't always accurate. At Point du Hoc, an American Ranger division battled their way up steep cliffs to take out what was believed to be a huge battery, but when they reached the top, the German guns had already been removed, and the many who had lost their lives in the effort, had in effect been sacrificed unnecessarily.

What with the bad weather, the injuries already sustained, and the loss of equipment to the stormy sea, it could well have appeared that halfway through the first day of Operation Overlord, the landings were not achieving what had been hoped for. Nevertheless, this was a huge undertaking and the strength of Overlord always relied upon its scale, and by the end of June the 6th, over 156,000 Allied troops had successfully landed on the beaches and there were many more to come.

In no time at all, laden with equipment, troops began to move off the beaches and into the French countryside. By marching twenty or so miles inland the divisions were able to link up so that a massive beachhead could be formed, ready for the next step of the invasion plan.

On 7th June, the weather finally started to improve and as a result a great deal of equipment could now be brought onto the beaches, as the Allied troops swiftly neutralised the Nazi defences in the first few days of the landings. They were able to do this with relative ease because so many of the elite German forces were busy fighting the Allies in Italy and on the eastern front, with many of those stationed in Normandy being conscripted schoolboys with no military experience whatsoever.

Within hours, there was a steady flow of Allied soldiers into Normandy, and more were due to come. To help get reinforcements and supplies ashore as quickly as possible the men got to work straight away on the construction of the Mulberries, the specially constructed floating harbours. These colossal sea structures extended right out into the channel and helped to get men and equipment onto the beaches in almost any weather condition. Today you can still see the remains of the Mulberry built at Gold Beach in the British sector, but the one at Omaha was actually destroyed in the bad weather.

As well as the sea route, the landing force also had to make sure that there were safe locations for planes to land and take off from. Temporary airstrips were constructed and were quickly operational. After the initial upsets everything seemed to be going to plan and the troops were pouring onto the beaches in Northern France. By the 14th of June there were over half a million soldiers on the beaches of Normandy, and despite the hardships faced by the Allied troops, not least the appalling weather, the landings had been a triumphant success.

For the Allied leaders, especially Eisenhower, who had taken full responsibility for Operation Overlord, in the face of Winston Churchill's misgivings, the relief must have been immense. It is interesting to note that sometime later, after Eisenhower had announced to the world that Operation Overlord had succeeded, a speech was found, probably written by Eisenhower on the morning of June the 6th, which simply said that Overlord had failed and the troops, whether army, navy, or air force, were not to blame, and the fault, if there were any, lay totally with him.

As French towns along the Normandy coastline were steadily liberated and Hitler's reign of terror was coming to an end, the German Fuhrer was still capable of unleashing his anger on the British, from where the Invasion had come. Hitler had always promised his people a secret weapon and the Nazis were in desperate need of such a devise if they stood any chance of fighting back after D-Day. The weapon he unveiled was the V1 flying buzz bomb, and the world had seen nothing like it before, and initially it was able to devastate many targets in London.

The V1 was an unpiloted rocket that could be launched from sites across mainland Europe, over the Channel to Britain, Hitler's intended target. The bomb was a technological marvel and those not sent running in fear of the bomb were awestruck by this devastating, yet seemingly futuristic devise. Luckily, despite the initial panic they caused, many of these bombs were shot down before they hit their targets and only a third of the

2,452 V1s launched in June ever reached their destination. Although the bomb was causing a number of casualties, Germany could not produce and launch the numbers of VI bombs needed to cause any real problem for the British at this late stage in the war.

Even though the V1 was not going to win the war for the Germans, the troops in Normandy were still extremely concerned at what was going on back in Britain. They wanted to waste no time in breaking out of their beachhead as quickly as possible to end the war before more damage was done to their loved ones back home.

In the early weeks after the D-Day landings the Allies were able to advance quickly into France because the Germans still believed that this was a diversionary tactic and the main attack was still to come at Calais, giving the Allied forces the time to link divisions and head out into Normandy. The Americans headed to the northwest region of France where they were able to take control of the port of Cherbourg, which meant further troops and supplies could be brought in safely.

The British, with General Montgomery at the helm, marched towards Caen, but this proved to be a much harder fought battle, as the invasion force finally met with much stronger Nazi opposition.

The Germans had eventually mobilized their forces to meet the Allies and a month of heavy fighting dominated the Caen end of the landing area and Monty's troops suffered some serious losses at the hands of the Germans. The British armoured divisions lost 200 tanks and were not able to breach the determined German defences. Monty knew his first attack had failed and had to call his men back to rethink tactics. However although the Allies may have lost this battle, Monty knew it was nothing compared to the size of the whole operation, and they could still win the war.

It was mid-July and there were now over a million men who had landed on the beaches of Normandy and because of these huge numbers, Allied divisions could be sent to fight anywhere they were required.

So Monty decided to keep the German divisions busy fighting in the North of France around Caen, keeping the American forces clear to be able to head south, where they faced little or no opposition, allowing the Allies to ease into a position where they could attack the Germans from the rear. The Nazis may have been determined to beat the D-Day invasion back into the sea, but they were woefully outnumbered and as the weeks passed, it became evident that they were the ones that now needed a miracle if they were to stand any chance of holding onto France as an occupied territory.

There was also great news from Russia, as by the 31st of July the Red Army were only 12 miles from the Polish capital of Warsaw. In fact as early as April 1944, the Russians had recovered almost all of their pre-war territory and were working hard to liberate other countries in Europe. The Red Army were now far superior to the fleeing Germans and with the second front underway in France, Stalin knew it was only a matter of time before the Nazi army would be completely crushed.

The Americans had also made many significant advances in the Pacific as well, and in the summer had occupied a vital territory, which would enable them to directly attack the home islands of Japan. For the Allies, the American fighting forces took the important Saipan islands in the Marianas, which were only 1200 miles away from Tokyo, which allowed their B-29 bombers to launch safely and begin bombing raids on Japan.

For the first time since Japan entered the war, the Allies could now directly attack their homeland, and while the Allies in Europe got ever closer to Germany, the Axis powers of evil, that even at the beginning of 1944 had still appeared an impossible enemy to overcome, were now seriously facing defeat on all sides.

Hitler was clutching at straws to stay in the war now, it had been months since a successful counterattack had been launched and his troops on every front were retreating. In the Pacific, the Japanese were being pushed back and the campaign that they had launched in India was failing to make any headway. In Europe, the Germans were being pushed further and further towards Berlin, as the Russians on the eastern front and the British and Americans in the west, began to close their net around Hitler and his troops, wherever they happened to be.

By the end of August, after another unsuccessful counterattack from the Germans, the battle for France had been all but won. Nevertheless 300,000 German military personnel were able to escape from France before the Allies cut off the Falaise pocket, but they had to leave behind ordnance and equipment, just as the British Expeditionary Force had done way back in 1940, when the had escaped from the beaches of Dunkirk.

The Germans by now realised that they were seriously outnumbered, and having neither the manpower nor equipment to stay in control of France, they retreated back to the German border to take up their defensive position. Victory in the battle of France was now in sight for the Allies, and the French people could at last look forward to regaining their freedom after so many years under Nazi occupation.

Two million Allied soldiers made their way through France, liberating the nation as they went, however despite many of the Germans having surrendered, there were still pockets of Nazi resistance in the country. By September, the Germans had lost

500,000 men and the Allies half that number, with fighting still intense in places, and although many believed that the war had now been won, towards the end of September the Allies, under Montgomery's command, were given a stark reminder as to why the Nazis should never be underestimated.

The Allies suffered heavy losses as a result of Operation Market Garden, a mission aimed at securing the many bridges in Belgium, to create a clear path all the way to the North German plain. It was a risky operation because it meant stretching the Allied troops very thinly, however the rewards would have been great, accelerating the end the war, in effect providing a short cut into Germany.

Unfortunately, the Allies cut too many corners, and the Germans penalised them severely for this. In the end Monty had to call the offensive off as the Nazis refused to relinquish their positions, and only 2,500 of the 10,000 Allied soldiers involved in the mission survived or evaded capture to fight another day.

The Allied commanders learnt a costly yet important lesson at Arnhem, because even in defeat, the Nazis could still inflict terrible damage. When Operation Market Garden was launched the paratroopers were dropped over three separate days in small consignments, but this meant the British 1st Airborne division never overwhelmed the Germans at any stage, and the result was a lost opportunity. Up until this point it was thought that the war in Europe would be over before the end of 1944, but Operation Market Garden taught the Allies that there was no short cut to victory.

As autumn turned to winter the worsening weather slowed down the Allied offensive to a crawl. Instead of trying to cross the River Rhine, following the Nazis, who had retreated back to Germany, Allied command judged it safer to let the troops hold their position until the spring and then made one final push towards Germany. Montgomery even wanted to go home for Christmas, believing that an Allied victory was a foregone conclusion.

However, again the Allies were underestimating the enemy, and Hitler came up with one last major counterattack, that would prove very costly indeed. The Fuhrer's strategy was not dissimilar to his invasion of France way back in 1940 when he attacked the enemy from behind their defensive lines. Hitler gathered together 600 tanks and 200,000 men ready to attack through the Ardennes, recapture Antwerp and then hopefully split the Allies in two, and push them back towards the sea, just as he had at Dunkirk.

It was a high-risk strategy, and Hitler's dwindling resources meant he was someway short of the numbers of men and tanks required for the mission to succeed. But Hitler was by now anything but rational, and would without doubt fight to the last, launching his attack on the Allies on 16th of December.

The attack at first took the Allies totally by surprise, it had been planned in complete radio silence, so even with Ultra, British Intelligence had failed to intercept any information. Consequently, the Battle of the Ardennes, forever known in popular culture as the Battle of the Bulge, proved conclusively that the Nazi war machine still had a sting in the tail.

The Americans were thrown into panic and confusion as the Germans attacked, and the majority of the casualties inflicted on the US divisions during the entire battle were sustained in the first three days. Hitler really believed as 1944 drew to a close that he had a fighting chance of forcing the Allies to negotiate a peace treaty in favour of the Axis powers.

That Hitler was losing what little grasp he had left on reality by this stage, is without doubt, and as the war headed towards a climax the human suffering of those who had already lived through six years of conflict, worsened dramatically at the hands of the desperate Nazis. Like a wounded animal Hitler's regime was very dangerous indeed, and although there was hope on the horizon for the Allies, there was still a great deal to be done if the threat posed by the Nazis was to be removed, once and for all.

Nevertheless, the people of Britain knew that the war was coming to an end, as the home guard was discharged, and pre-war streetlamps were replaced. Thoughts of loved ones returning and the prospect of a New Year bringing the promise of peace, was the best Christmas present anyone could have hoped for, not only in Britain, but in Allied nations, the whole world over.

WORLD WAR II HISTORY JOURNALS: 1945

Although the Allied nations faced the New Year of 1945 with a huge sense of hope, there was still a great deal of work to be done if world peace were to become a reality. Adolf Hitler and his Axis powers were finally facing defeat after seven years at war, but just like any wounded animal in the wild, they continued to pose a very real and dangerous threat.

The all-important D-Day landings in June 1944 had been an unprecedented success, and the ground forces who had breached the German's costal defences were steadily moving through France, liberating towns and villages as they went, gathering momentum as they set their sights on Berlin. To say that the Germans and Japanese were out of the war would be premature, but the time was fast approaching when the Axis reign of terror would be over.

As 1944 had drawn to a close, Adolf Hitler had unleashed what would prove to be his last major counter-offence of the war, in what become known as the Battle of the Bulge, fought amongst the French forests of the Ardennes. As many tanks as the German commanders could muster, along with 250,000 men, were engaged in a desperate attempt to push the Allies back into the sea, exactly as had happened at Dunkirk back in 1940, and the fight continued as the days of January passedMeanwhile, the Japanese were not in a position where they could fight back so fiercely.

In the Pacific, the Americans were starting their New Year celebrations by continuing to advance towards the Japanese homeland. On 1st January, the US Navy launched more attacks on Japanese islands to increase their superiority in the area, by air, land, and at sea. The Japanese were desperately using any means at their disposal to try and beat the Americans back, from Kamikaze pilots to suicide submarines. For the Japanese, with an ancient culture that permitted no surrender, they would die with honour rather than survive as prisoners, and this was very dangerous indeed for the Allies.

But to make matters worse for the Axis powers, and Hitler in particular, the Russians were already beginning a major winter offensive. They were concentrating their forces in Poland, ready for a big push into Warsaw. Hitler was unsure as to where the Russians would choose to strike, so consequently he had to place divisions, very thinly spread, all over the Eastern front.

As a result when Russia instigated an attack on the 12th of January, the Nazis were hugely outnumbered. 2.2 million Russians stormed towards Warsaw on two separate flanks, to be faced by a mere 400,000 Germans hoping to stop them, and it was by now apparent that Nazi Germany was fast running out of options. In fact during this particular attack the Russians had an advantage of almost 8 to 1 in Guns, 6 to 1 in tanks and 18 to 1 in aircraft as well as superior manpower, making the outcome a foregone conclusion.

Nevertheless, back in the Ardennes, Hitler's campaign could not be dismissed so easily. The Battle of the Bulge had proved a tough fight for the Americans because the Allies had not had any warning from military intelligence.

Even so, once the element of surprise was countered by some fierce fighting, with the American soldiers on the ground enduring some horrifically cold conditions, the Germans were unable to capitalise on their early advantage. On the 7th of January, Hitler withdrew his forces from the Ardennes, and the Battle of the Bulge went down in history as a decisive victory for the Allies when it was concluded on the 25th . However, Eisenhower had another battle to resolve in the aftermath, which would take every bit of tact and diplomacy he could muster.

After the breakout from the Normandy beachheads following the D Day landings, the then British General, Bernard Montgomery had wanted to take command of operations in France, but Eisenhower had elected to take that very important role himself. In a conciliatory gesture Winston Churchill had promoted Monty to the rank of Field Marshal, but the tensions between Montgomery and the Americans escalated.

When Hitler withdrew from the Ardennes, Montgomery held a Press Conference claiming that teamwork had won the day, giving no credit to the American Generals Patton and Bradley, who had undoubtedly been responsible for the victory. In fact when Eisenhower had requested that Montgomery go on the offensive on the 1st of January, Monty chose to ignore him waiting until the 3rd to act, by which time a significant number of Germans escaped to fight another day.

Patton and Bradley threatened to resign if Eisenhower didn't do something about Montgomery, although it's highly probable Monty had no idea how much resentment he'd caused with the Americans, dating right back the North African campaigns and Italy. In the end Montgomery apologised and Eisenhower was able to move forward with all his key people still in placeThis was just as well, because after the shock of the Battle of the Bulge, they had to replenish their divisions ready to continue the long push towards Germany. The Allies had lost 81,000 men and over 733 tanks in the operation, but it took just two weeks for them to get back to strength. However for the Nazis, who had sustained similar losses, the consequences were catastrophic. Not only were they unable to call in reinforcements, but the operation had also taken troops away from the fighting in Poland. Hitler's last gamble had definitely not paid off, and what is more, had put him under even more pressure.

So as expected, on the 17th of January the Red Army stormed through Poland and captured Warsaw. Hitler had enslaved Warsaw for over five years and the devastation was appalling. There would be much rebuilding to be done in Europe in years to come, but for the time being, the most important thing was for the Red Army to continue their unrelenting march towards Berlin. Advancing more than 100 miles a week, by the beginning of February they had crossed the German border and were only 45 miles from Berlin. The end was in sight.

And at the same time the Allies on the Western front were also closing in on Berlin.

But Montgomery was still causing problems with the American Generals by wanting all their efforts to be secondary to his command. Eisenhower, who after all had successfully landed four million men in Normandy and liberated France, stuck to his original plan. He proposed an advance to the Rhine and then when the Allied troops had successfully crossed the river, they would take control of the Ruhr. Yet before they could do this, they would have to deal with the German troops stationed to the west of the Rhine. On the 8th of February, the Americans began their Rhineland campaign, while the British and Canadian troops headed for the Siegfried Line, a defensive German border that ran from Holland in the north to Switzerland in the south.

The American troops were also progressing well in the Pacific and in February set their sights on the Volcanic Island of Iwo Jima. This was another crucial island, as even though it was only eight miles square, it was in a prime location to attack Japan from.

Iwo Jima is only 750 miles south east of Tokyo and from here fighter escorts could take off to protect the bombers heading for Japan. The Japanese also knew the importance of this island

and had 21,000 of their elite soldiers stationed here to protect it. The Japanese considered every possible way to keep the Americans off Iwo Jima and even discussed the quantity of explosives needed to sink the island into the sea.

Because Iwo Jima was so vital to both sides, it became a desperate battle for the tiny island, resulting in serious casualties all round. However four days into the fighting the Americans sensed victory, and marines from the 28th Regiment famously lifted the Stars and Stripes on Mount Suribachi.

With a flagpole made out of a discarded drainpipe, the soldiers hoisted the flag on the peak after they had fought and scrambled their way up to the 167-metre summit. The raising of the flag gave hope to millions of people around the world and especially to the soldiers still locked in this bloody battle.

Everywhere the marines looked they could see fellow soldiers who had been killed, and although the war may have been close to ending, the casualties continued to pile up. Even though the Americans had lifted the flag in victory, the Japanese continued to fight and by the end of the six-week conflict. as many as 7,000 Americans had been killed, while only 216 Japanese soldiers were taken alive.

Back in Europe, the Allies were making great advances towards the crossing of the Rhine. Hitler's attempts to defend the Rhineland were another disaster and after several weeks of fighting, even the Fuhrer had to concede after losing quarter of a million men. The Germans were down to their last reserves, so the order was given for a retreat across the Rhine. Hitler decreed that no bridge should be left intact, so as to hinder Allied progress, and when they reached the river, they found almost every crossing had been destroyed. Although this failed to stop the Allies from crossing, it would buy Hitler some precious time to reassess his defences.

Unbeknown to Hitler, a troop of disorganised Nazis were caught fleeing an intact bridge near Remagen, to the south of Germany. The Ludendorff railway bridge needed some repair, but the American engineers soon got the bridge operational again, allowing men and tanks across to cross as the Allies quickly surrounded the 300,000 Germans in the Ruhr pocket.

Over in the Pacific the Americans, although victorious, were still nursing their heavy losses on Iwo Jima. However as soon as they organised a stronghold, they wasted no time in using the island to their advantage. As they continued to bury their dead, hordes of B-29 bombers took to the skies to begin an all-important raid over Tokyo. On the 10th of March, 83,000 Japanese people were killed in the bombings, with over 1 million being made homeless.

After these attacks, the Americans planned their invasion of Okinawa, another strategically important island, a mere 340 miles from Japan. The Americans were aware that if the Japanese were prepared to defend this 60-mile island as fiercely as they did the tiny island of Iwo Jima, they would need to be very well prepared.

In Europe, the progress of the Allies was slowing down, in part because there was little communication between the Russian troops in the East and the American, Canadian and British forces in the west, however towards the end of March this all changed. Montgomery and Churchill wanted to make a push for Berlin, yet Eisenhower took a different view. Churchill was concerned that Stalin would exploit the political advantage of being the first to reach Berlin and Montgomery believed the Western Allies who were experiencing less resistance than the Russians, could get to Berlin quicker.

But Eisenhower did not want to risk the lives of his men, for

Churchill's political gain. Berlin was Hitler's city and Eisenhower knew that the fight ahead would be bloody and costly. So to minimize losses and keep the Russians onside, he promised Stalin the grand prize of Berlin, while the Western Allies would concentrate on the North of Germany, much to the chagrin of Montgomery and Churchill.

By this stage in 1945, Germany had lost almost all of the territories gained since the beginning of World War II. Hitler's 1,000-year Reich was tumbling as the Allies now attacked from both sides. The Russians were preparing for their last march on Berlin as the Western Allies crossed the Rhine in droves. Even so, the resistance they met was still at times unpredictable. At some crossings, the enemy immediately surrendered, while others would fight to the last bullet. The only certainty was that the German Empire was collapsing bit-by-bit, and day-by-day. Communications were down, supplies low and the Nazis had become more frantic than ever.

Defeat was now inevitable, and Hitler, accompanied by his entourage, had sought shelter in an underground bunker in Berlin since the middle of January, refusing to flee, despite advice from his commanders, to his mountain retreat in Bavaria.

Yet Hitler still believed that his Empire could be saved and when Josef Goebbels brought news of the death of American President Franklin D Roosevelt, he actually congratulated Hitler and told him it was the turning point they had been waiting for. Roosevelt died on the 12th of April at the age of sixty-three. The whole of America mourned the loss of the Democrat who had helped lead the nation out of the economic recession of the 1930's before turning his attention to World War II.

Many couldn't believe that he died so suddenly, with America and the Allies on the brink of victory, and Harry S. Truman, quickly sworn in as the 33rd American President, had a very hard act to follow.

The reason for the Nazi's optimism was the belief that Roosevelt held the Allies together and without him the conflict between the supposedly united nations could just give Hitler the room for manoeuvre he needed. But the Nazis were clutching at straws, the Americans, British and Russians may have had many different political views, but they were determined to finish what Hitler had started.

A few days before Roosevelt's death, the first American troops landed on the Pacific Island of Okinawa, and while shocked and saddened by the news, they were determined to honour President Roosevelt's memory. Within an hour of the invasion there were 160,000 Americans on the island, and by 10am they had already taken control of two airfields. The Americans expected heavy opposition to Operation Iceberg and so gathered a huge invasion force to deal with the resistance of 120,000 Japanese soldiers.

But when the American invasion vessels landed, the beaches were strangely empty. The Japanese were clever fighters and stationed the bulk of their men far enough inland to be out of range of the American's deadly naval guns, and they gave everything to defend their island, including deploying many Kamikaze pilots to attack the invaders.

Despite the tenacity of the Japanese the bigger picture for the Axis powers was about to make their position a great deal weaker. The Russians were so close to achieving their aims in Europe they announced their intention to join the Americans in the fight against Japan in the Pacific:

This signalled to the Japanese that the Russians were ready to attack, and Japan's North Western borders were now in danger. This was very bad news indeed as the Japanese were struggling to keep Americans at bay, so speculation that Russia was about to enter the Pacific war caused great concern in the Far East.

Contrary to what Hitler and the remaining Nazis had thought, the Western Allies in Europe were continuing to work well together without Roosevelt, as victory was now well within their grasp. Even the most respected Nazi publication, the Schwarze Korps, the newspaper of the SS, no longer hid the fact that the end was near, acknowledging that it was possible that the Germans could be defeated militarily. The article that revealed this shocking news went on to state that they would continue to fight, but with the reported surrender of over 100,000 Nazi soldiers in the Ruhr, whether the soldiers on the ground were of the same opinion is debatable.

The Germans were down to their last reserves and almost out of raw materials and fuel, but despite the Allies smelling victory, many Nazis undoubtedly in desperation, were determined to take as many of the enemy down as possible before they were killed. As a consequence the Americans lost 10,677 fighting men in April 1945, almost as many as they lost the previous year when the German forces were much stronger. The Reich may have been disintegrating, but it was fighting to the last man.

But by now the Allies in Europe knew that all they had to do was maintain their advances and sooner or later the Nazis would fall.

The confidence of the Western Allies was so apparent that they now opened another offensive on the Italian front to ensure that their impending victory would be as widespread as possible, and with the help of Italian partisans they met very little resistance from the dwindling Nazi presence. The same was also true in Germany itself with military personnel fast disappearing, as the Nazi troops were forced further back towards Berlin.

Hitler's mental state and capacity for rational thought was deteriorating at an alarming rate. His master plan of a New World order was being crushed, so he demanded that the German people destroy their nation before the enemy got a chance to. He simply couldn't face the humiliation of Germany, as he perceived it, for a second time in his lifetime, but fortunately for the German population, this was one order that his commanders were not prepared to carry out.

As the war was coming to an end more of the atrocities committed by the Nazis were being discovered. It was back in January when the Russians liberated the infamous death camp at Auschwitz, and the allies were now making daily discoveries of the Nazi's crimes against humanity.

Far worse than the dead bodies that littered the battlefields, were the gaunt corpses that the Allies found in the death camps. Eisenhower and the other commanders were deeply affected by what they saw in these camps and if further incentive was required to remove Hitler from power as quickly as possible, then this was it.

On 14th April, the last push to end the war in Europe finally began. The task of taking Berlin now turned into a race for three of the Russian commanders and Stalin gave them two weeks to finish the job. The Russians were well prepared to take Berlin, with over three million men, 6,250 tanks and 7,500 planes. The Nazis by contrast, had hardly anything left to defend their most prized city with.

Their mighty Panzer division only numbered about 1,000 in Berlin, their planes 3,300 and with a meagre 320,000 soldiers, boosted by a million German civilians in the people's militia, there was little hope. Yet the Germans were determined to fight on to the very end, just as Eisenhower had predicted, and the

Red Army did suffer a huge number of casualties as they fought a vicious street-by-street battle.

With the Russians literally about to storm Hitler's bunker the Fuhrer's final hours included marrying his long-term mistress Eva Braun on the 29th of April. Although they had been together for many years Hitler had always been reluctant to marry Eva, believing that the affair needed to be kept secret so as not to upset his adoring female supporters. But evidently with no way out of the Bunker, marrying Eva Braun was the last act of a desperate man.

Then the very next day, the 30th of April, after a dinner shared with his two favourite secretaries Hitler retired to his private room with his bride, and the newlyweds committed suicide. Eva ended her life with a lethal dose of poison while Hitler, also took poison, and shot himself. His thousand-year Reich was over, in little more than twelve.

Without their Führer, the other commanders in the bunker knew there was no hope for them. Many committed suicide, some tried to escape, others tried to negotiate peace, while a few fought on until it was all over. The German forces in Italy had already surrendered to the Western Allies, the Americans and Russians had linked up on the River Elbe and other Russian divisions were pounding Berlin into the ground. The Western Allies had won the battle of the Ruhr taking 325,000 prisoners; they had done their job and now all they had left to do was wait until the Red Army took Berlin, which would ensure an unconditional Nazi surrender.

Stalin as we already know gave his Commanders two weeks to secure Berlin and every indication was that this would be the length of time it would take. The Russians, after breaking down the outer resistance, formed a ring around the city and swiftly moved towards its heart. Berlin was subject to constant shelling from the Russians, backed up by Russian planes to destroy pockets of German resistance.

The RAF also helped in the raids and together they smashed the city, totally encircling Berlin, leaving no way out for the Nazis. The Russians doggedly completed their task, taking street-by-street, house-by-house. Not only were the Germans low on manpower, weapons and fuel, by this stage they also had no food, and their only option was to surrender to the Allies.

On the 4th of May 1945, in a military tent on the Luneburg Heath, three generals and two admirals reluctantly signed the surrender of all German armed forces in North West Germany, the Netherlands and Denmark. As Field Marshal Bernard Montgomery read out the terms, an extremely nervous looking German General tried to light a cigarette.

Monty, who disapproved of smoking strongly, gave the General a sharp look and the German quickly, and with no argument, put the cigarette away. The once mighty Nazi pride had been well and truly tamed. The surrender was scheduled to take effect from 8 am on the 5th of May, with over half a million troops involved. But there were still pockets of fighting and the RAF continued to carry out attacks on German U-Boats to hammer home the message that the war in Europe was over, and with so many troops already surrendered, peace was literally hours away.

At 2.40 am on the 7th of May, General Alfred Jodl, of the German high command, signed the surrender of all German forces, whether fighting on land, at sea or in the air. The General then asked that the victorious Allies treat the vanquished Germans with respect; however, with all that the people of Europe had endured, especially those nations occupied by the Nazis since the beginning of the conflict, very few of them could find much generosity of spirit to show towards the Germans.

In fact, in Great Britain, the population was so keen to celebrate the end of the war in Europe, the parties started a day earlier than had actually been scheduled. Western journalists broke the wonderful news prematurely, and VE Day, planned for the 9th of May, was celebrated in Britain on the 8th. To this day Russia and a number of other European countries still commemorate Victory Day on the 9th of May, while in Britain it's always the day before.

As the sun rose on a nation that had survived the threat posed by Adolf Hitler for seven years, with the promise of peace and the return of all those servicemen who had lived through the horrors of war, the community spirit that Hitler had failed to break was once more in evidence on VE Day 1945. Tables and chairs were dragged out into the streets, Union Jacks were flying everywhere, and somehow sandwiches and cakes were produced for tea parties, despite strict rationing still being very much in place.

The church bells rang out in towns and villages the length and breadth of the country, but when most people think of VE Day, it's the celebrations in London that first spring to mind. Crowds gathered from Trafalgar Square, down the Mall, all the way to Buckingham Palace, where the King, George the Sixth and Queen Elizabeth stepped out on to the balcony to share the joy of their people. Prime Minister Winston Churchill joined the Royal family, where he received the grateful adulation of a nation he had led through the dark days of war, into a brave new world.

When Churchill gave a victory speech from 10 Downing Street, he managed in a few eloquent words to sum up the feelings of the British, looking forward to future peace.

The German war is at an end. Advance Britannia! Long

live the cause of freedom! God save the King.

Churchill made many announcements throughout VE Day, however amongst the celebrations his thoughts turned to those still locked in combat out in the Pacific, where all eyes now turned:

Finally almost the whole world was combined against the evildoers who are now prostrate before us. But let us not forget Japan, with all her treachery and greed, remains un-subdued and her detestable cruelties call for justice and retribution.

Peace may have come to Europe, but the Allies were still duty bound to carry on fighting until an uncompromised peace was achieved in the Pacific, where the US Navy continued to bear the brunt of Japan's refusal to consider surrender.

The Americans had lost their leader, Franklin D Roosevelt, less than a month before VE Day, and as Europe celebrated, the USA was still in mourning for their beloved president. The man charged with continuing the fight, President Harry S Truman, who celebrated his 61st birthday on VE Day, dedicated the victory in Europe to his predecessor.

As a mark of respect for Roosevelt, who had worked so tirelessly, despite ill health, to end the war, the flags still flew at half-mast until the end of the official mourning period on the 12th of May. The task ahead of President Truman was immense, and as the true enormity of the situation became apparent, the world watched and waited, as history was made.

As VE Day came and went, the American forces were still tied down on the island of Okinawa.

Since the US landings in April, well over five weeks previously, the Japanese had increased their attacks using Kamikaze pilots in a desperate attempt to force the Americans off the island.

1,092 suicide bombers had already died for the cause and it certainly appeared that many more would follow. The Americans however were continuing to advance, but at a painfully slow 120 metres a day, sustaining heavy casualties, having lost in the region of 20,000 soldiers since the invasion began.

The Japanese were tenaciously prolonging a fight that they had no hope of winning, and with a culture that demanded death with honour, it was impossible to calculate, even at this stage, how long the war would actually go on for.

Elsewhere, Japanese troops were now being withdrawn from a number of Chinese ports, some of which they had only held for a very short period of time. Since the Americans had captured the Philippines, these Chinese ports were within bombing range, and Japan knew that it needed to save as many fighting men as possible, which could be best achieved back in Japan.

This was a major concern for the Allies, as fighting the Japanese anywhere was a tall order, but on home territory they would be even more difficult to overcome. The cost in terms of Allied servicemen could be huge, and to gather together an invasion force capable of smashing the Japanese war machine would take considerable time and planning. The Western Allies were also concerned by the Russian involvement in the Pacific.

The British and American governments were wary of what the Russians might do if they occupied Japan, and there was already enough diplomatic disagreement about the handling of post-war Germany, let alone bringing the islands of the Far East into the fray as well. The relationship between the Western Allies and the Russians had always been strained, but they had at least united in their common fight against Hitler, to settle their differences.

But now with Hitler out of the equation, the political differences were now glaringly obvious, with America and Britain being capitalist and democratic societies while the Russians were communist and authoritarian. And Stalin's record on human rights was equally as bad as Adolf Hitler's had been.

Wherever the Red Army was in control throughout Europe, Czechoslovakia, Poland, Bulgaria, Hungary and Romania, one-party regimes, under Russian control were storming to power. If Russia were able to take control of Japan as well, the United Nations feared that an end to World War II might not herald a peaceful future, and the threat of fighting breaking out again on a global scale, would be a distinct possibility.

So the Western Allies faced a dilemma, they had to work together to beat the Japanese, without allowing the Russians to gain too much ground. Stalin had promised that his troops would help the Allies smash Japan within ninety days of there being peace in Europe, nevertheless the Americans had an alternative plan they had been working on for some time. It was a secret weapon that they believed could quickly and decisively end the war with Japan.

What's more, peace in the Pacific could be achieved without Russian involvement, and with the minimal loss of American servicemen, but it was a final solution that would come at a very high price in terms of humanity.

In the last three years before his death, Franklin D. Roosevelt had supported the top-secret Manhattan Project, which was working towards the development of an atomic bomb. Involving 120,000 people, at a cost of 2 billion US dollars, the Manhattan project was so secret that even Harry S Truman, as Vice President, knew nothing about the nuclear program until he was sworn in as Roosevelt's successor. By the summer of 1945, the Americans had three atomic bombs ready for deployment, requiring only the go ahead from President Truman to unleash the ultimate weapon of destruction on the Japanese.

By the end of June, the Americans had won the battle for Okinawa, with as many as 90,000 Japanese soldiers having lost their lives. Tens of thousands of Japanese civilians had also been killed and almost all of the senior officers involved had committed ritual suicide. Losses for the Americans were also devastatingly high with 7,000 dead, 32,000 wounded and 26,000 non-battle casualties, many of whom had suffered breakdowns as a result of what had been a truly barbaric conflict.

But their efforts had not been in vain, Japan was now on the verge of total collapse.

Most of the nation's merchant fleet had been sunk, US ships now constantly patrolled the Japanese coastline, industrial production was at a standstill and the constant bombing raids from the Americans meant that internal communications had been destroyed, while the Japanese people were facing starvation.

With Germany out of the war, the Americans knew that beating the Japanese was simply a matter of time, but with a proud warrior culture, there was every chance it could be years rather than months. Preparations were made for the Allies to land in Japan using three massive invasion plans, codenamed Olympic, Coronet and Zipper, and although the Americans knew this would bring them victory, the cost in Allied losses could be huge.

The Americans only needed to look back to Okinawa for proof of what the Japanese were capable of. Also they felt the Russians could not be trusted on Japanese soil, leaving President Truman forced to consider using atomic warfare to ensure an unconditional Japanese surrender.

On the 16th of July in the New Mexico desert one of the three nuclear bombs was successfully tested. The bomb exploded with a destructive force comparable to 20,000 tons of TNT and the light emitted was visible from over 125 miles away. Mankind had produced a weapon like nothing ever seen before, the power that it possessed was unimaginable, and once unleashed the Americans, as its creator, knew it would change the world forever.

Meanwhile in Britain, enjoying the first months of peacetime, there had already been significant changes, because on the 26th of July a General Election resulted in Winston Churchill and the Conservatives being voted out of power, in favour of Clement Atlee and the Labour Party.

Winston Churchill, the man who had epitomised the spirit of the British people in the war against Adolf Hitler, who on the balcony at Buckingham Palace just a matter of weeks earlier had received the adulation of the nation he had led through some of its darkest hours, was dismissed as Prime Minister. Churchill simply said, *"I thank the British people for many kindnesses shown towards their servants"* ending an era that would never be forgotten.

As Churchill left office in Britain, the recently appointed American President, Harry S Truman had made a momentous decision, giving the Japanese an ultimatum. If they did not surrender before the 3rd of August, America would deploy the atomic bomb. Leaflets were dropped over Japan stating that people should 'flee or perish', but still there were no sign that a surrender was imminent, and Truman was as good as his word.

At 8.15am on the 6th of August the American B-29, Enola Gay, piloted by Colonel Paul Tibbets, drooped the first atomic bomb on the city of Hiroshima. As the great mushroom cloud billowed into the sky, 60,000 people were killed instantly, with thousands more dying in the weeks to come as a result of burns, injuries, and radiation. People were scorched in seconds where they stood, birds vaporised in the sky and entire buildings ceased to exist.

For the Americans involved, the bomb had been a complete success and they were overjoyed at what they had achieved. At first there was very little sympathy for the Japanese because of the terrible atrocities committed by their soldiers during so many years at war.

After the bomb exploded and the debris settled, the Russians officially declared war on Japan and marched more than a million and a half Soviet soldiers towards China, but the Americans did not want the Red Army going any further. With still no sign of a Japanese surrender the order was given to drop another atomic bomb on the 9th of August. Nagasaki was the second target, and 40,000 more lives were instantly lost in the blast, with many more dying day after day as a result of the radiation.

For Japan's leaders it was dishonourable to surrender, but they could no longer ignore the devastating power of this new weapon.

On the 14th of August 1945, the Japanese Emperor recorded a message for the people of Japan, it was the first time anyone outside of his court had heard his voice, and he explained why surrender had been the only option:

Despite the best that has been done by everyone...the war situation has developed not necessarily to Japans advantage...moreover the enemy has begun to employ a new and most cruel bomb, the power of which to do damage is indeed incalculable, taking a toll of many innocent lives. Should we continue to fight, it will not only result in the obliteration of the Japanese nation but also it would lead to the total extinction of human civilization.

With these words, World War II came to an end, after seven years of bitter conflict. Now a formality, American troops landed in Japan and accepted the formal surrender on the 2nd of September. With Truman's announcement this marked Victory in Japan, or VJ Day, and people all over the globe celebrated that world peace had finally been restored.

Peace however came at a terrible price, and every nation involved in the conflict, whether Axis or Allies, would need many years to recover and rebuild. Over 50 million lives were lost in the fighting, with homes destroyed and countryside decimated everywhere that war touched. Europe was awash with refugees, and many of the countries that had been occupied by the Nazis found it hard to rebuild a diplomatic government. Reprisals could be vicious and brutal, as ten million Germans fled their homes in the aftermath, to avoid Russian vengeance.

Hitler's years in power had changed the landscape of Europe beyond all recognition, and although the years of recovery would be incredibly difficult, the alternatives would have been a great deal worse. People may have lost everything, their loved ones, their homes and their personal possessions, but the one thing they had regained was freedom and the right to live, worship, work and speak as they chose. It would take years, decades, and perhaps even centuries for the wounds to heal, but the words of General Douglas Macarthur spoken after receiving the official surrender from Japan, expressed what so many were feeling as 1945 came to its historic conclusion.

It is my earnest hope, indeed the hope of all mankind, that from this solemn occasion a better world shall emerge out of the blood and carnage of the past, a world founded upon faith and understanding, a world dedicated to the dignity of man and the fulfilment of his most cherished wish for freedom, tolerance, and justice.

And what more appropriate note could there be to end this series of War Journals on? This journey of discovery has taken us from the outbreak of war in 1939 right through to its conclusion in 1945. We have followed the twists and turns of military strategy and all the elements of good and bad fortune; there were times when a victory for the Axis powers looked inevitable, as Adolf Hitler appeared invincible.

But wherever you look in the history books, sooner or later those who disregard the rights of their fellow man rarely stay in power forever, as humanity has a unique ability to fight back. In the case of World War II, the lessons of history, as you have now read here, have been recorded for posterity through the power of pixels and hopefully in this new media age, they are lessons that will never be forgotten.

❖ ❖ ❖

WOULD YOU PLEASE CONSIDER LEAVING A REVIEW?

Just a few short words would help others decide if this journal is for them.

Visit www.amazon.com and your "Orders" page where you can leave your comments and thoughts.

Best regards and thanks in advance.
Liam Dale

◆ ◆ ◆

FURTHER JOURNALS & BOOKS BY LIAM DALE

WW2; The Call of Duty - A complete timeline
The War Diaries 1939-1945 (7 titles)
Mary Queen of Scots
Alexander the Great
King Arthur
Richard the Lioneheart
Boudicca - Warrior Queen
Marie Antoinette
Jack the Ripper; Victims and Suspects
Winston Churchill - His finest hour
Wartime Britain
Napoleon
America in WW2
D Day - The Normandy Invasion
Princess Diana
Catherine Cookson
The Brontes
D.H. Lawrence
Thomas Hardy
Jane Austen
Hannibal
William Shakespeare
Sir Arthur Conan Doyle (Sherlock Holmes)
Marie Antoinette
Chaplin - The life and time
Jack the Ripper - In the footsteps
Royal Romances - The British Monarchy
Charles Dickens - Master of his own destiny
Royal Scandals & Conspiracies
Attack on Pearl Harbor
Frankin Delano Roosevelt
Troy - For Love & War

Robin Hood - The Outlaw Hero
The Kings & Queens of Great Britain
William Wordsworth
Bram Stoker
The Rise & Fall of Adolf Hitler
Why Hitler lost WW2
Mary Shelley - Mother of Frankenstein

◆ ◆ ◆

ABOUT THE AUTHOR

Liam Dale is a unique character in the world of books, film, and television, who has the ability to write, produce, present and direct at the highest level. Whatever the subject matter, Liam's honest, down to earth, creative journalistic vision brings an extra dimension to any story, making even the most traditionally academic or limited special interest topics accessible to a far wider audience.

From Jane Austen to ancient steam trains, ghosts and witches to giant fish species, Alexander the Great to WW2, Liam Dale's style is synonymous with quality entertainment, enlightening, delighting and amusing to equal measure.

Printed in the USA
CPSIA information can be obtained
at www.ICGtesting.com
CBHW070431140824
13125CB00038B/629

9 798746 158284